WOOD PELLET SMOKER AND GRILL COOKBOOK

The Ultimate Wood Pellet Smoker and Grill Cookbook

Aron Jones

derived from various sources. Please consult a licensed professional before attempting any techniques outlined in this book.

By reading this document, the reader agrees that under no circumstances is the author responsible for any losses, direct or indirect, which are incurred as a result of the use of information contained within this document, including, but not limited to, — errors, omissions, or inaccuracies.

TABLE OF CONTENTS

INTRODUCTION

Today, pellet grills are the protagonists in the world of barbecues and grills. Everyone is excited about the different features and conveniences that pellet grills are acquiring. Obviously, to appreciate its qualities, it is important to understand how they work. So, if you don't know the pellet or smoke grills yet and you don't know how they work, then you are reading the right book!

WHAT IS A PELLET GRILL?

A revolutionary type of barbecue is spreading on the market that allows you to cook food in a healthy way and with the same tastes and smells that you get with wood cooking: the pellet barbecue. Working exclusively with specific pellets for cooking food (the best qualities are oak, alder and beech pellets), this type of barbecue is equipped with cutting-edge technology that allows you to grill a wide range of foods, such as bruschetta, meat, fish, vegetables and pizzas, in a fast, practical way and with optimal results.

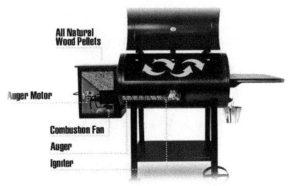

HOW DO THE PELLET GRILLS WORK?

(Components of a pellet barcecue: steel construction=steel structure, porcelain coated grill= porcelain grill, pellet hopper= pellet tank, convection blower=convection air blower, auger=clochea, auto start firepot=automatic fire start, drip system=fat collection dryer, smoke exhaust=channel for smoke exhaust).

Generally the modern pellet barbecue models are equipped with:

Power supply: the power of medium sized barbecues is about 230 V

Automatic switch-on: Pressing the on button starts the appliance and the brazier starts to heat up;

Electronic thermoregulator: regulates the flame and temperature, keeping them constant;

Porcelain grill: ensures maximum hygiene and is easy to clean, there are also examples with stainless steel grill;

Electronic control panel: allows to select the type of cooking and the desired temperature in a simple and fast way;

Ventilation system: ensures uniform cooking of food and, since the grill is separated from the brazier, the flame never comes into contact with food and there is no risk of flames or propagation of benzopyrene, a highly toxic substance that can be generated when cooking using coal or gas;

Drip tray: it is a small bucket for collecting the fats that melt while the food is cooking; this type of cooking, called indirect, is considered very healthy by dieticians, as the food dries excess lipids, without losing its authentic taste;

Stainless steel lid: covers the grill and protects the food;

External display: allows you to see the degree of cooking achieved without opening the lid;

Rubber wheels: to comfortably transport the barbecue.

The barbecue is switched on immediately after pressing the start button. At that point the pellets, which are contained in the hopper on the side of the appliance, descend into the brazier through a stick and the flame is fed by a device that blows convection air. Usually it only takes a few minutes to reach the selected temperature, for example to reach 240 degrees, it takes only 15 minutes. As far as consumption is concerned, larger pellet barbecues burn, on average, half a kilo of pellets per hour, with a 10 kilo bag you can cook for about 5 times, so the pellets are cheaper than gas and coal.

WHAT DO THE PELLETS LOOK LIKE?

Pellets, classified as biomass, have the shape of small cylinders created by pressing wood waste with special plants, allowing the binding through lignin, the constituent substance of wood, without the addition of additives, solvents and glues harmful to human health and the environment.

Following the pressing process, the pellets, while still hot, are cut to the desired length and passed to the cooling process in special compartments, at the end of which the pellets are sifted through dust and remains, to ensure a percentage not exceeding 1% according to current regulations.

It is precisely the pressing process that gives the pellets a double energy density compared to natural wood, generating the property of higher caloric yield and optimal combustion, whose ashes can still be used as fertilizers, further renewing the process of exploitation of the energy resource.

HO LONG DO PELLETS LAST IN A PELLET GRID?

It would be correct to have 2 kilos of pellets per hour of slow smoking or 4 kilos per hour of hot and fast grilling.

WHY GRILLS WITH PELLETS?

The various types of pellets used therefore produce a smoke which thus aromatizes the food.

That's why many use pellet grills as a simple alternative to traditional smokers.

Some manufacturers of pellet grills have implemented controls via Wi-Fi thanks to which it is possible to have grill remote monitoring. Pellet grill technology has been integrated into other cooking devices, such as traditional Kamado-style ceramic grills and pizza ovens.

PELLET GRILL / SMOKER

A pellet barbecue is extremely easy to use, being able to set both the desired cooking temperature and the time. The pellet also, burning homogeneously, creates much less residues than coal, which translates into more cleaning and easier maintenance of the product. Although the starting cost is higher than the charcoal barbecue, this is recovered over time thanks to the price of the pellet, which although of quality, is still cheaper than coal. The argument of the best smoking of the dishes with coal is then, as we have seen, only partially true. Thanks to the lid of the barbecue itself and the possibility of choosing pellets of pure compositions (you can still experiment by mixing different types), it is possible to achieve satisfactory levels of smoking although not comparable to those of coal. In addition to this there is the speed of use. The pellet in fact, although it is not able to reach the same temperatures as the coal, still manages to heat the plate or the grill in a few minutes, making the barbecue ready for use in a time much less than that required for the preparation of the barbecue charcoal.

In conclusion it is possible to say that the pellet barbecue is an ideal product for those who want to give their dishes the taste of wood without excessively getting their hands dirty with coal or firewood. For those who love the taste of dishes cooked over a flame but do not want to manage the drawbacks of temperature regulation or subsequent cleaning. In other words, the pellet barbecue has all the advantages of a charcoal barbecue (or almost) and none of its defects, making it a product in perfect line with today's times, where time is money. Pellet grills can eliminate this frustrating task, making the smoking process practically "set and forgotten". Therefore you can enjoy the benefits of the taste of smoking without having to be a barbecue expert.

Pellet grills also offer the convenience of combining several cooking options into one unit.

PELLET GRILL / PROPANE (GAS) GRILLS

Pellets and propane both offer the possibility to "set it and forget it", but this is where the similarities end.

The first obvious difference between a propane smoker and a pellet smoker is the fuel they use.

Pellet smokers use wood pellets. These pellets are generally made from hardwood ground into sawdust and then compacted into pellets through the use of heat and pressure. The main advantage of using a pellet smoker is that they use wood as fuel, which provides its smoky flavor.

They also tend to be quite high-tech with companies like Traeger and Green Mountain Grills offering models with Wi-Fi so you can control them with an app from the comfort of your sofa.

The main disadvantage of a pellet smoker is the price, which can range from $500 to about $1800. Pellet grills are also quite voluminous and generally need to be connected to an electrical outlet.

The availability of fuel is also a concern, as the smoker only works with pellets and these can cost up to $2 per kilo.

It is not surprising that propane smokers escape from a propane tank. Compared to a pellet smoker, propane smokers are simple to use and easy to repair. Propane and propane accessories are readily available in many stores.

The main advantage of a propane smoker is the ease of use and the fact that you can get similar results to a traditional coal smoker.

The main disadvantage of propane smokers is that gas fumes are known to add a slight flavor to meat. However, how much this affects the taste seems to be somewhat subjective, with some claiming that they are unable to taste it at all.

PELLET GRILL / CHARCOAL GRILL

As far as ease of use is concerned, there is no doubt that the pellet barbecue is designed specifically for those who have no time to waste and who want to dedicate themselves immediately to cooking the food. The pellet barbecue is in fact extremely easy to use. The procedure is as simple as it sounds. You have to fill the special container with pellets (the one specifically designed for cooking food) by pressing the start button, and set the desired temperature. At this point the pellets contained in the special container will be automatically fed into the brazier to have a hot plate or grill ready to use in a few minutes. The consistency of the pellets also guarantees even cooking and an adjustable temperature through the special electric control panel. For the coal barbecue, however, things are not so simple. In addition to having to feed the flame manually, it is much more difficult to maintain a constant temperature for as long as it takes to cook food, not to mention the fact that a coal barbecue is much slower and requires a preparation time of several tens of minutes before it is operational and ready to use.

Temperatures are also another element to be taken into consideration for those who decide to buy a new barbecue. The real strength of the pellet barbecue is, in fact, as has already been noted, the ability to keep the cooking temperature constant for as long as necessary, and have the peak performance at low temperatures, which are easy to reach and maintain thanks to the type of fuel and the ability to set them to our liking. As far as high temperatures are concerned, on the other hand, the pellet barbecue has more limits than the coal barbecue, which can easily reach around 500 °C compared to the 300 °C of pellets.

PELLET GRILL / ELECTRIC SMOKER

This is the easiest barbecue to use because you just plug it into a power outlet. The grill is heated by a heating element and all you have to do is wait for the ideal cooking temperature to be reached. Another advantage offered by the electric barbecue is that it does not smoke, so you can use it at home if you wish. As for the excess smell, simply place the barbecue under a fume hood or ventilate the room after you have finished cooking. One disadvantage of this type of barbecue is the consumption of electricity, which can be quite high, depending on how you use it. Finally, the taste of food cooked with an electric barbecue is not at all comparable to that obtained with a classic wood or coal barbecue.

WOOD PELLET SMOKER AND GRILL RECIPES

POULTRY

STUFFED SMOKED TURKEY

Prep Time: 1hr Cook Time: 3hrs Total Times: 4hrs
Serving: 6

INGREDIENTS

- ✓ 15lb Whole Turkey
- ✓ 1 cup Kosmo's Turkey Brine
- ✓ 1 gallon Water
- ✓ Killer Hogs AP Seasoning
- ✓ Swine Life Miss Grind Rub
- ✓ 14oz Pepperidge Farm Seasoned Bread Cubes
- ✓ 1 lb Country Sausage
- ✓ 22oz chicken broth
- ✓ 1 cup Granny Smith Apple
- ✓ 1 cup Celery
- ✓ 1 Onion
- ✓ 3 cloves Garlic
- ✓ 1 stick Butter
- ✓ 1 large Egg
- ✓ 2 T-Spn Killer Hogs AP Seasoning
- ✓ 1 teaspoon fresh Rosemary
- ✓ 1 teaspoon fresh Thyme
- ✓ 1 teaspoon fresh Sage

INSTRUCTIONS

1. Defrost turkey and take giblet p.C. And neck. Spot Turkey in XXL plastic ziplock stockpiling percent, Add 1 cup Kosmo's Turkey Brine and 1 gallon of water, press the permit a few streams into of sack and close. Spot the turkey in a huge plastic bowl or tote and see it inside the cooler for 24Hrs.

2. Take the turkey out from the saline answer and permit plentiful fluid to use up away. Air to dry the skin tapping it with a paper towel to take out dampness.

3. In a big sauté skillet darkish to colored wiener and channel. Leave 1 Tbl-Spn of wiener drippings inside the field and sauté onion, celery, and apple for 3 to fourmins. Include garlic and prepare dinner for a further 2mins.

4. Splash the skin with cooking shower and season with Killer Hogs AP Seasoning observed by Swine Life Mississippi Grind.

5. In a large bowl join the bread three to D shapes with a wiener, sautéed combination, liquefied spread, egg, herbs, 1 teaspoon AP flavoring and bird juices. Mix to sign up for and stuff into the pit of the turkey. Tie the legs collectively with butcher twine to keep within the stuffing.

6. Set up a pellet flame broil for circuitous cooking at three hundred levels utilizing a blend of Hickory, Maple, and Cherry wooden pellets for boosting.

7. Spot the turkey at the smoker and cook till an internal temperature of 165 inside the bosom. Make certain to check the inward temperature of the stuffing too. It likewise needs to arrive at 165 previous serving.

8. Take the turkey out from the smoker, rest for 15mins before slicing.

HERB BUTTERED SPATCHCOCK CHICKEN

Prep Time: 1omins Cook Time: 1hr Total Times: 1hr 10mins   Serving: 3

INGREDIENTS

- ✓ 1 stick of butter
- ✓ 2 tbsp. garlic powder
- ✓ 2 tbsp. chipotle chili powder

SEASONING

- ✓ Thyme
- ✓ Basil

INSTRUCTIONS

1. Begin with a sharp butcher blade and start by scoring a line down the center of the spine. When you have your score line, press solidly into the winged creature and cut it down through the center. Rehash the whole procedure on the

opposite side. In the wake of evacuating any additional fat, spread the chicken open so it lays level.

2. To make your infusion flavoring, start by dissolving 1 stick of margarine and emptying it into a blending bowl. Next, include 2 Tbl-Spn of garlic powder and 2 Tbl-Spn of chipotle bean stew powder. Whisk the entirety of the fixings until very much joined.

3. Fill your flavoring injector and infuse 2 to 3 infusions into the bosom until you feel it start to grow. Additionally, make certain to infuse season into the thighs and legs. Next, sprinkle the highest point of your chicken with thyme and basil, to taste.

4. Set your Grilla to 275^0 and place your chicken on the meshes. Leave the smoker shut for 45 to seal in the juices and take on the smoke. After the underlying 45mins, check the inward temperature and wrench your warmth up to 350^0 for one more hour. Presently, check the inner temp. by and by to ensure that the entirety of the parts hit 165^0.

5. Spot your chicken on a slicing board and permit it to rest for a couple of mins to secure the entirety of the juices. Wrap up by cutting your chicken for serving and appreciate!

CHIPOTLE STYLE SMOKED THE WHOLE TURKEY

Prep Time: 40mins Cook Time: 3hrs Total Times: 3hrs 40mins   Serving: 8

INGREDIENTS

- ✓ Kosher Salt
- ✓ Cumin
- ✓ Adobo Chipotle
- ✓ Oregano
- ✓ Granulated Garlic
- ✓ Chili Paste

- ✓ Chili Powder
- ✓ Ancho Chili Powder
- ✓ Olive Oil Spray
- ✓ Butter
- ✓ Whole Turkey (15 lbs)

INSTRUCTIONS

1. To begin, take a pointy blade and spatchcock your chook. For those who do not have the foggiest concept of the way to investigate this video for an into profundity explanation.

2. When the backbone has been Takeled, clean out your winged animal and coat it in a flimsy layer of an authentic

salt. When included, bathe a light layer of olive oil splash onto your feathered creature in an effort to preserve your seasonings adhered to your turkey.

3. Next pour on any of the thicker fixings like bean stew glue or adobo chipotle glue and gently rub them on over the entire turkey. Presently, pour a decent measure of the remainder of the dry seasonings, for example, cumin, oregano, granulated garlic, and bean stew powder. Try not to unfold or rub the seasonings as on the way to make it cluster and give lopsided flavor. Each flavoring or sauce can be carried out for your very own taste to level.

4. Presently, take a bit spoon or dessert scoop and make balls from your margarine. They should every be usually the scale of a ping pong ball. Contingent upon the size of your flying creature, you could require somewhere in the variety of 6 to 10 fatsos.

5. Next, make a little reduce close to the neck of your winged creature in an effort to lightly pull the skin far from the meat. Don't completely evacuate the pores and skin, basically raise it sufficiently high to can help you slide the chunks of margarine between it. Close to the thigh joints, either facet of the bosom and the focal point of the turkey are ideal spots to begin. Put forth a valiant effort to keep them similarly spread during the chicken.

6. Once sufficiently prepared, positioned your turkey for your Grilla Grill at normally 275º. Leave it in for approximately

45 to 50mins, at that factor knock the temperature as much as 350⁰ for the closing hour of cooking. These occasions are for a fifteen lbs fledgling, so change as wishes be for the dimensions of your turkey. Your Thanksgiving chook ought to arrive at an inner temperature of in any occasion 165⁰ for secure utilization.

GRILLED BBQ ORANGE CHICKEN

Prep Time: 10mins Cook Time: 20mins Total Times: 30mins   Serving: 7

INGREDIENTS

- ✓ 1 whole 5 to lb (or larger) chicken
- ✓ 1 24 to oz jar orange marmalade
- ✓ 1 TB fresh ginger
- ✓ 2 TB red pepper flakes
- ✓ ¼ C Grilla AP Rub
- ✓ 3 TB Grilla BBQ Sauce

INSTRUCTIONS

1. In the occasion that you need to spare prepare dinner time, you may want to start via dispatch to positioning the hen. This will reduce round 20 percentage off of the cook time. In the occasion that you lean closer to the creation of an entire bird depart entirety. Preheat your Grill to 275°.

2. In a bit sauce skillet, melt the orange jelly on low. Include the BBQ sauce and ginger to this mixture.

3. Coat the chook with the rub and spot on the fish fry. On the off threat that you dispatch cooked the winged animal, begin with the pores and skin to the facet equipped for cooking. Flip the fledgling over in part thru cooking. On the off threat which you left it complete, at that factor you will cook bosom to side up for the entire prepare dinner.

4. Your cooking time will change contingent upon the size of the flying creature, but, you need to cook until all portions of the winged animal arrive at an internal temp of 165^0. In the event that you plan on pulling the beef separated, at that point, you need to take the temp to at any rate 175^0. Your whole prepare dinner time for an entire feathered creature might be actually over 2Hrs.

5. During the remaining 20mins of cooking, cowl the winged creature with the jelly combination in 10 to 12mins interims. In the occasion that you have some last, that is great—it is outstanding to dunk the meat into on the off chance which you pull the beef from the flying creature.

SMOKED TURKEY LEGS

Prep Time: 7hrs Cook Time: 20mins Total Times:
7hrs 20mins   Serving: 4

INGREDIENTS

- ✓ 8 Turkey Legs
- ✓ 2 quarts water
- ✓ 1/2 cup Sugar
- ✓ 1/2 cup Killer Hogs AP Rub
- ✓ 2 to 3 Bay leaves
- ✓ ¼ cup Killer Hogs The BBQ Rub
- ✓ 1 cup Killer Hogs Vinegar Sauce

INSTRUCTIONS

1. In big bowl join water, 1 cup sugar, ¼ cup AP rub, and narrows leaves. Spot the turkey legs into the saline solution arrangement and refrigerate medium-term or possibly 6Hrs.

2. Take the legs out from the saline solution and channel over a cooling rack. Pat the overabundance dampness off with paper towels to speed the procedure.

3. Get ready smoker for aberrant cooking at 275^0 utilizing walnut wood for smoke.

4. Shower the outside of every leg with olive oil cooking splash and season with the remaining AP rub and a light covering of The BBQ Rub on all sides.

5. Spot the legs on the smoker and cook until interior temperature arrives at 155 to 160^0.

6. Coating every turkey leg with the vinegar sauce and keep on cooking until the inside temperature arrives at 175^0 at that point Take from the smoker and rest for 5 to 10mins before serving.

BACON CANDY CHICKEN BITES

Prep Time: 30mins Cook Time: 1hr 45mins Total Times: 2hrs 15mins   Serving: 4

INGREDIENTS

- ✓ 16oz Boneless, Skinless Chicken Thighs
- ✓ 12 slices Bacon (cut in half)
- ✓ ½ cup Brown Sugar
- ✓ 2 Tbl-Spn Killer Hogs The BBQ Rub
- ✓ 2 Tbl-Spn Turbinado Sugar
- ✓ ½ teaspoon Cayenne Pepper

INSTRUCTIONS

1. Get ready Smoker or Grill for backhanded cooking at 375^0
2. Slice every thigh into chomp to measure parcels. Wrap each piece with ½ cut of bacon and secure with a toothpick.
3. Consolidate the darker sugar, bar-b-que rub, turbinado, and cayenne in a little bowl and sprinkle over all sides of the bacon to wrapped chicken.

4. Spot the chicken chomps onto the barbecue and cook for about 45mins or until the bacon is totally darker and clingy.
5. Present with your most loved plunging sauces.

MONTEREY CHICKEN

Prep Time: 5mins Cook Time: 20mins Total Times: 25mins   Serving: 6

INGREDIENTS

- ✓ 4 Chicken Breast (boneless/skinless)
- ✓ 2oz Grande Gringo Mexican Seasoning
- ✓ 12oz Bacon (crumbled)
- ✓ 4oz Monterey Jack Cheese
- ✓ 4oz Sharp Cheddar Cheese
- ✓ 1 cup Killer Hogs BBQ Sauce
- ✓ 2 to 3 Green Onions (chopped)

INSTRUCTIONS

1. Get ready pellet flame broil for cooking at 325^0 utilizing Cherry wood pellets for fuel.

2. Season the chicken bosom with the Grande Gringo Mexican flavoring on all sides.

3. Spot the bosoms on the pellet flame broil, embed a test thermometer to screen inner temperature.

4. At the point when the inside temp arrives at 155 exchange the chicken bosoms to a level iron skillet and coating with Killer Hogs BBQ Sauce. Keep on cooking the bosoms until the inner arrives at 165^0.

5. Top each bosom with disintegrated bacon, cheddar, and jack cheddar. Return the skillet to the barbecue and cook for 3 to 5mins or until the cheddar liquefies over the top.

6. Enhancement the Monterey Chicken with green onions and serve.

PORTERHOUSE STEAK

Prep Time: 5mins Cook Time: 20mins Total Times: 25mins   Serving: 4

INGREDIENTS

- ✓ 2 24oz porterhouse steaks
- ✓ Big Poppa Smokers Cash Cow
- ✓ Killer Hogs Steak Rub
- ✓ Steak Butter
- ✓ Steak Butter
- ✓ 1 Stick of Butter
- ✓ 2 to 3 Cloves Roasted Garlic
- ✓ ½ Tbl-Spn Shallot

Slice

- ✓ ½ tea fresh Thyme
- ✓ ½ teaspoon fresh Sage
- ✓ ½ teaspoon fresh Rosemary
- ✓ 1 teaspoon Kosher Salt
- ✓ ½ teaspoon Cracked Black Pepper

INSTRUCTIONS

1. Season porterhouse steaks with Big Poppa Smokers Cash Cow on the 2 sides and permit 10 to 15mins for flavoring to infiltrate the meat.

2. Get prepared fish fry for high warmth flame broiling at 450 to 500⁰. Barbecue Grates are discretionary however will assist steak with cooking similarly and bring higher flame broil marks.

3. Season porterhouse steaks with Killer Hogs Steak Rub on the 2 sides.

4. Spot steaks legitimately on a barbeque and delicately push all the way down to guarantee wonderful touch.

5. Flame broil steaks for 4mins every aspect topivoting a part of the way thru to supply crosshatch marks.

6. Flip steaks and rehash a comparable procedure.

7. Utilizing a test thermometer test the internal temperature and Remove steaks from flame broil when they have come to the correct doneness.

8. Spot 2 faucets of Steak Butter on a platter and set completed steak straightforwardly on top for a 10 to 15min relaxation.

9. Spot steak on slicing board and pour the relaxation of the Steak Butter Dipping Sauce into a bit bowl and serve

SMOKED TURKEY TACOS

Prep Time: 5mins Cook Time: 70mins Total Times: 75mins   Serving: 4

INGREDIENTS

- ✓ 1 Bone to in Turkey Breast
- ✓ 1/4 cup Mexican style seasoning
- ✓ 1 Tbl-Spn olive oil
- ✓ 1 medium yellow onion
- ✓ 6 cloves garlic
- ✓ 4 chipotle peppers in adobo sauce
- ✓ 28 oz diced fire to roasted tomatoes
- ✓ 14oz chicken broth
- ✓ 2 Tbl-Spn ground oregano
- ✓ 1 Tbl-Spn salt
- ✓ 2 T-Spn ground cumin
- ✓ Jalapeño Lime Slaw Recipe
- ✓ 1/2 head cabbage finely shredded
- ✓ 1/4 cup cilantro finely chopped
- ✓ 1/4 cup green onion chopped
- ✓ 1 jalapeño diced
- ✓ 1/4 cup mayonnaise
- ✓ 1 Tbl-Spn Red wine vinegar

- ✓ 1 Tbl-Spn Yellow
  Mustard
- ✓ 1 Tbl-Spn vegetable oil
- ✓ Juice from 1/2 lime
- ✓ Zest of 1 lime
- ✓ 2 T-Spn white sugar
- ✓ 1 teaspoon salt
- ✓ 1 teaspoon black pepper
- ✓ 1/2 teaspoon ground
  oregano
- ✓ 1/2 teaspoon ground
  cumin

INSTRUCTIONS

1. Consolidate the cabbage, cilantro, jalapeño, and green onion in a huge bowl. In a different bowl include the mayo, mustard, vinegar, oil, and straining fixings. Speed to consolidate and pour over cabbage blend. Toss to join and refrigerate for in any event 60mins.

2. Take overabundance dampness out from Turkey by leaving behind a paper towel. Shower skin with canola oil and season with Mexican style dry flavoring.

3. Get ready smoker for roundabout cooking at 225⁰. In any case, utilize your preferred wood for smoke season.

4. Spot the turkey bosom on the smoker and cook for 60Secs low and slow. Increment the temperature to 300⁰ and keep on cooking until interior temperature arrives at 165 on a test thermometer.

5. Freely spread the turkey with aluminum foil and rest at room temperature.

6. In a big pot over medium warmth include 1 Tbl-Spn of olive oil and cleaved yellow onion. 6. Cook for 2 to 3mins or until onion mellow. Addminsced garlic and keep on cooking for 2 to 3mins.

7. Include oregano, cumin, and hacked chipotle peppers and cook for 3 to 4mins. At that point add fire to cooked tomatoes, chicken stock, and salt.

8. Carry the sauce to a stew and lessen it for 5 to 7mints.

9. Transfer the sauce into a nourishment processor and mix until smooth.

10. Shred the turkey bosom into a cast iron pot, include the sauce and toss delicately to cover.

11. Spot the cast iron pot on the smoker revealed for 30mins. Wrap tortilla shells in aluminum foil and spot on the smoker nearby the turkey during the last 5mins.

12. For serving spread out the tortilla shells and layer with the destroyed turkey. Top with Jalapeño Lime slaw, cotija cheddar, salted red onion, or any of your preferred taco garnishes.

LAMB

LAMB SHOULDER CHOPS

Prep Time: 5mins Cook Time: 2hrs 10mins Total Times: 2hrs 15mins   Serving: 4

INGREDIENTS

- ✓ 4 Lamb Shoulder Chops 1" thick
- ✓ 2 Tbl-Spn Kosher Salt
- ✓ 2 Tbl-Spn Corse Ground Black Pepper
- ✓ 2 Tbl-Spn Fresh Rosemary chopped fine
- ✓ 1 Tbl-Spn Lemon Zest[SEP]
- ✓ 4 Cloves Garlicminsced
- ✓ 1/4 cup Olive Oil
- ✓ Braising Liquid:

- ✓ 1 Onion cut into strips
- ✓ 4 Cloves Garlicminsced[SEP]
- ✓ 2 Tbl-Spn Butter
- ✓ 1 Tbl-Spn Olive Oil
- ✓ 1 Tbl-Spn Fresh Rosemary chopped fine[SEP]
- ✓ 1 Cup Red Wine
- ✓ 1 Cup Beef Broth
- ✓ 1 Cup Chicken Broth

INSTRUCTIONS

1. Sprinkle Lamb Shoulder Chops with Olive Oil. Join Kosher Salt, Black Pepper, Rosemary, Garlic, and Lemon Zest in a little Bowl. season each slash on the two sides.

2. Plan wood terminated pellet flame broil or another comparative barbecue for aberrant cooking at 325⁰ utilizing cherry wood pellets or pieces for the smoke season.

3. Spot sheep on barbecue surface and cook for 60Secs flipping after 30mins to dark-colored the two sides.

4. In a dutch stove or broiling skillet include olive oil and spread. Cut the onion into strips and darker in the dutch broiler for 5 to 7mins.

5. Include garlic, rosemary and cook an extra 2 to 3mins. Pour in Red Wine, Beef Broth, and Chicken Broth and bring to a stew. Lessen the fluid and spot each hack in the dutch broiler once sautéed. Spread and cook for 2 1/2Hrs or until fork to delicate. Serve family to style over pureed potatoes or rice.

JACK DANIELS RIBS

Prep Time: 10mins Cook Time: 4hrs 30mins Total Times: 4hrs 40mins   Serving: 3

INGREDIENTS

- ✓ 2 slabs St Louis Spare Ribs
- ✓ 2 Tbl-Spn Killer Higs Hot Rub
- ✓ 2 Tbl-Spn Swine Life MS Grind
- ✓ 1/2 cup Brown Sugar
- ✓ 1/4 cup Captain Rodney's Boucan Glaze
- ✓ Jack & Coke Spritz
- ✓ 8oz Coca Cola

- ✓ 2oz Jack Daniels TN Whisky
- ✓ Pint jar of Ice
- ✓ Jack Daniels BBQ Glaze
- ✓ 8oz Brown Sugar
- ✓ 8oz Killer Hogs Vinegar Sauce
- ✓ 2oz Jack Daniels Whisky
- ✓ 2oz Pineapple Juice

INSTRUCTIONS

1. Join fixings and permit the blend to come to room temperature before setting in a spritz bottle

2. Consolidate fixings in a sauce container over medium warmth until darker sugar breaks up. Keep on warming until blend arrives at a slight bubble and decrease warmth to stew. Cook for 5mins and permit to cool before coating ribs.

3. Get ready pellet smoker or flame broil for aberrant cooking at 250^0 F utilizing hickory pellets for smoke enhance.

4. Take film and abundance fat out from every chunk of ribs.

5. Season with a light to medium layer of Mississippi Grind followed by a layer of Hot Rub.

6. Spot ribs on smoker and cook for 2 1/2 hrs spritzing with Jack and Coke blend varying.

7. Take ribs out from the smoker and spot on a twofold layer of aluminum foil. The spread portion of the dark-colored sugar on the foil followed by 1 to 2 Tbl-Spn of Boucan Glaze. Spot ribs meat down right now wrap with foil.

8. Spot every section back on the smoker for 1/2Hrs or until delicate.

9. Cautiously unwrap the foil and brush each side with Jack Daniels Glaze.

10. Keep on cooking ribs for 15 to 20mins until coat sets. Take it out from the smoker, rest for 5 to 10mins, and serve.

BLUE CHEESE BISCUITS

Prep Time: 25mins Cook Time: 18mins Total Times: 33mins   Serving: 12

INGREDIENTS

- ✓ 2 cups Self Rising Flour
- ✓ 1 Tbl-Spn Baking Powder
- ✓ 1 3/4 cup Buttermilk
- ✓ 1 stick of Unsalted Butter grated
- ✓ 1 teaspoon sugar
- ✓ 4oz Blue Cheese crumbled
- ✓ Pinch of Salt
- ✓ 3 Tbl-Spn Butter melted (optional)
- ✓ 2 teaspoon Dried Parsley (optional)

INSTRUCTIONS

1. Prepare grill for indirect cooking at 425⁰.
2. Combine Flour, Baking Powder, Salt, & Sugar in a mixing bowl.

3. Add grated butter (keep it very cold) to Flour mixture and stir. Fold in Blue Cheese gently.
4. Pour in Buttermilk and stir mixture slowly until dough forms.
5. Turn dough out onto floured surface and roll into 1/2 thickness. Cut into biscuits.
6. Grease a cast to iron skillet with 1 1/2 Tbl-Spn canola oil.
7. Place biscuits in a skillet and cook for 25 to 30mins until brown on top and around edges.

REVERSE SEARED TRI TO TIP

Prep Time: 5mins Cook Time: 90mins Total Times: 95mins   Serving: 4

INGREDIENTS

- ✓ 3lb Tri to Tip Roast
- ✓ 1/4 cup Kosher Salt
- ✓ 2 Tbl-Spn Killer Hogs AP Rub
- ✓ 2 Tbl-Spn Killer Hogs Hot Rub
- ✓ 1 Tbl-Spn Coarse Ground Black Pepper

INSTRUCTIONS

1. Prepare pellet smoker or any other grill/smoker for indirect heat at 275⁰.
2. Trim excess fat from Tri to Tip (leave 1/4" fat on the bottom side if possible).
3. Season the Tri to Tip with Kosher Salt and rest for 8 to 10mins.

4. Rinse the salt off under cool water and pat dry with a paper towel.

5. Use a jaccard to tenderize the Tri Tip.

6. Season with AP, Hot Rub, snd Blsck Pepper.

7. Place tri tip on smoker and cook until internal temp reaches 115^0.

8. Prepare charcoal grill for direct searing at 600^0.

9. Seat Tri Tip for 3 to 4mins on both sides until internal temperature reaches 125 or your desired doneness.

10. Once Tri Tip hits doneness, wrap in butcher paper and allow to rest for at least 10mins.

11. Slice across the grain and serve.

SMOKED LOBSTER MAC & CHEESE

Prep Time: 20mins Cook Time: 60mins Total Times: 80mins   Serving: 4

INGREDIENTS

- ✓ 1.5lb Lobster Tails
- ✓ 8oz Elbow Macaroni
- ✓ 16oz Milk
- ✓ 1 stick Unsalted Butter
- ✓ 1/4 cup All to Purpose Flour
- ✓ 1 cup Sharp Cheddar Cheese grated
- ✓ 1 cup Gruyere cheese grated
- ✓ 1 cup Mozzarella Cheese shredded
- ✓ 1/2 cup Panko Bread Crumbs
- ✓ Juice from 1/2 Lemon
- ✓ 2 T-Spn Killer Hogs AP Rub
- ✓ 1 teaspoon Killer Hogs Hot Rub
- ✓ 1/2 teaspoon Old Bay Seasoning
- ✓ 1/2 Teaspoon Ground Nutmeg
- ✓ 1/2 teaspoon White Pepper

INSTRUCTIONS

1. Prepare a pellet smoker or any grill/smoker for indirect cooking at 300. Place lobster tails on the smoker for 15 to 20mins until meat turns opaque.

2. Prepare elbow macaroni according to package instructions.

3. In a medium to size sauce pot melt butter over medium heat. Add milk and flour and until whisk until smooth and simmer is reached.

4. Add Gruyere, Cheddar, and Mozzarella cheeses. Stir until cheese melts.

5. Add seasonings and lemon juice. Keep warm until ready to combine.

6. Chop lobster tail into bite to size portions. Place macaroni, lobster, and cheese sauce in a 5qt Dutch oven. Stir to combine, adjust seasoning if necessary.

7. Top with remaining cheese and Panko bread crumbs.

8. Place on the smoker at 300 for 25 to 30mins or until the top is brown

GRILLED PINEAPPLE UPSIDE DOWN CAKE

Prep Time: 30mins Cook Time: 93mins Total Times: 2hrs 3mins   Serving: 6

INGREDIENTS

- ✓ 1 can pineapple sliced
- ✓ 1 jar Marciano cherries
- ✓ 3/4 cup light brown sugar
- ✓ 1 stick of butter (halved)
- ✓ 1 1/2 cups flour
- ✓ 1 cup white sugar
- ✓ 1 cup buttermilk
- ✓ 2 large eggs
- ✓ 1 Tbl-Spn Baking Powder
- ✓ 1/2 teaspoon salt

INSTRUCTIONS

1. Plan smoker or flame broil for aberrant cooking at 350⁰.

2. In a medium to measure iron skillet include 1/2 stick of liquefied margarine. Whirl the skillet so the margarine covers the sides and base equally. Sprinkle dark colored sugar around the base of the skillet.
3. Orchestrate pineapple cuts in a solitary layer and spot fruits in the focal point of each ring.
4. In a big blending, bowl consolidates the flour, sugar, heating powder, and salt.
5. Include buttermilk, eggs, and 1/2 stick of liquefied margarine. Whisk fixings to consolidate.
6. Take cake player into the iron skillet and spot it in the smoker. Cook for 45mins to 60Secs or until a toothpick embedded into the middle confesses all.
7. Take the cake out from the smoker and permit to cook for 5 to 10mins. Flip the cake onto a serving platter and serve.

STUFFED VENISON BACKSTRAP

Prep Time: 2hrs Cook Time: 25mins Total Times: 2hrs 25mins   Serving: 5

INGREDIENTS

- ✓ 1 to 2 Whole Venison Backstraps
- ✓ 8oz Cream Cheese
- ✓ 8oz Baby Portabella Mushrooms chopped
- ✓ ¼ cup Crumbled Bacon)
- ✓ 1 small Yellow Onion diced
- ✓ 2 Tbl-Spn Bacon Drippings
- ✓ ½ cup Flat leaf Parsley chopped
- ✓ 2lbs Bacon
- ✓ 2 Tbl-Spn Killer Hogs AP Rub
- ✓ 2 Tbl-Spn Killer Hogs The BBQ Rub

INSTRUCTIONS

1. Prepare Pellet Smoker or any other bbq grill for indirect cooking at 350^0. Add your favorite wood to the hot coals

for smoke flavor. In the pellet grill I use a combination of Pecan, Oak, and Cherry cooking pellets.

2. To prepare the stuffing sauté onions and mushrooms in bacon drippings over medium heat. Add to room temperature cream cheese. Fold in crumbled bacon and parsley.

3. Trim excess silver skin from venison backstraps and cut a slit down the length to butterfly it open. Be careful not to cut through the entire piece.

4. Season with AP rub and stuff with cream cheese mixture.

5. Wrap the outside with strips of bacon and season with Killer Hogs The BBQ Rub.

6. Place each backstrap on a wire cooling rack and set on the smoker.

7. Cook until internal temperature reaches 130^0 or your desired doneness. The bacon should be brown on the outside.

8. Allow the backstrap to rest for 10mins and cut into individual pieces for serving.

MOLASSES GLAZED SALMON

Prep Time: 10mins Cook Time: 10mins Total Times: 20mins   Serving: 4

INGREDIENTS

- ✓ 2 Sockeye Salmon filets cut into 4 to 6oz portions
- ✓ 8oz Molasses Glaze
- ✓ ¼ cup Pastrami Rub
- ✓ Molasses Glaze
- ✓ ¼ cup Molasses
- ✓ ¼ cup Dark Soy Sauce
- ✓ 2 Tbl-Spn White Cooking Wine
- ✓ pinch of Red Pepper Flakes
- ✓ Pastrami Rub

- ✓ ¼ cup Coarse Ground Black Pepper
- ✓ 2 Tbl-Spn Kosher Salt
- ✓ 2 Tbl-Spn Turbinado Sugar (Raw Sugar)
- ✓ 1 Tbl-Spn Granulated Garlic
- ✓ 1 Tbl-Spn Coriander
- ✓ 1 teaspoon Ground Mustard
- ✓ 1 teaspoon Onion Powder

INSTRUCTIONS

1. Consolidate fixings in a little pot over medium warmth for 2 to 3mins whisking sporadically. Fill a little container or bowl and permit to cool before coating salmon.

2. Consolidate fixings in a little bowl and store in a water/air proof holder for as long as multi-month.

3. Preheat Traeger flame broil for backhanded cooking at 325^0 utilizing walnut pellets for the smoke season.

4. Brush each bite of salmon with Molasses Glaze and rest for in any event 30mins in the cooler.

5. Season the salmon filets with pastrami flavoring and spot legitimately on the cooking grate skin side down.

6. Cook until the inward temperature arrives at 135^0 in the thickest piece of each filet.

7. Take salmon from barbecue and rest for 5 to 10mins before serving.

SMOKED BREAKFAST CASSEROLE

Prep Time: 20mins Cook Time: 35mins Total Times: 55mins   Serving: 8

INGREDIENTS

- ✓ 2lbs ground pork sausage
- ✓ 1 cup Diced Onion
- ✓ 1 cup Diced Bell Pepper
- ✓ 1 cup Sliced Mushrooms
- ✓ 10 large Eggs
- ✓ 2 cups Shredded Cheese
- ✓ 1 cup Sour Cream
- ✓ 1 Tbl-Spn Hot Sauce
- ✓ 1 Tbl-Spn Butter
- ✓ 1 Tbl-Spn Olive Oil
- ✓ Salt and Black Pepper to taste
- ✓ 1 package Crescent Roll Sheet Pastry

INSTRUCTIONS

1. Dark colored hotdog over medium warmth and channel on a paper towel to lined platter.

2. Add spread and olive oil to dish and sauté vegetables until delicate around 3 to 4mins.

3. Consolidate hotdog and vegetables and put in a safe spot.

4. In an enormous blending bowl split eggs and whisk. Include cheddar, harsh cream, hot sauce, and a touch of salt and dark pepper. Race to consolidate.

5. Shower 9X11 inch heating skillet with cooking splash and spread bow move batter in the base.

6. Spread hotdog and vegetables over the batter equitably and top with egg blend. Rest the meal for in any event 60Secs in the fridge.

7. Set up a Traeger pellet flame broil or another smoker for cooking at 350^0.

8. Spot dish on bar-b-que pit and cook for 60Secs turning the skillet after 30mins for cooking.

9. At the point when the top is dark colored and edges pull marginally away from the skillet the meal is finished. Take ut from pot and cut into wanted serving sizes. Present with sharp cream, disintegrated bacon, pico, and so forth.

GENERAL TSO'S WINGS

Prep Time: 20mins Cook Time: 10mins Total Times:
30mins   Serving: 4

INGREDIENTS

- ✓ 3lbs Whole Chicken Wings
- ✓ ½ cup Killer Hogs AP Rub
- ✓ 2 Tbl-Spn Chinese 5 Spice
- ✓ 2 T-Spn Crushed Red Pepper
- ✓ 16oz General Tso's Sauce* recipe to follow
- ✓ General Tso's Sauce
- ✓ 1 cup Brown Sugar
- ✓ ½ cup Soy Sauce
- ✓ ½ cup Hoisin Sauce

- ✓ ½ cup Rice Vinegar
- ✓ ½ cup Water
- ✓ 1 Tbl-Spn Vegetable Oil
- ✓ 1 Tbl-Spn Sweet Chili Sauce
- ✓ 1 Tbl-Spn Crushed Red Pepper
- ✓ ½ Tbl-Spn Garlic Chili Paste
- ✓ 2 Tbl-Spn Green Onion chopped
- ✓ 3 cloves Garlicminsced
- ✓ 1 Tbl-Spn Fresh Gingerminsced

✓ 2 Tbl-Spn Cold Water   ✓ 2 Tbl-Spn Corn Starch

INSTRUCTIONS

1. Heat 1 Tbl-Spn of vegetable oil in a small saucepot over medium heat; sauté garlic, ginger, and green onion for 1 to 2mins.

2. Add the Soy Sauce, Hoisin sauce, rice vinegar, water, and brown sugar. Stir to combine

3. Stir in the sweet chili sauce, garlic chili paste, and crushed red pepper. Continue cooking until the mixture reaches a slight boil.

4. In a separate bowl combine the cornstarch and cold water. Slowly add the slurry to the saucepot while stirring. Bring the mixture to a boil and reduce the heat. Pour the sauce into a jar and allow to cool.

5. Prepare Yoder Smoker or another grill for indirect cooking at a temperature of 300⁰. Use cherry pellets for wood smoke.

6. Combine Killer Hogs AP Rub with Chinese 5 Spice and Crushed Red Pepper; coat both sides of the chicken wings with this mixture.

7. Place wings on the grill and smoke for 45mins then turn each wing over to evenly cook both sides.

8. After 60Secs 10mins glaze each wing with General Tso's Sauce on both sides and continue to cook until wings are

tender. Internal temperature should be at least 165⁰ and juice should run clear. Total Cook time about 1:20mins.

9. Arrange the wings on a large platter and garnish with Sesame Seeds and chopped green onion before serving.

SMOKED MEATLOAFMINSIS

Prep Time: 15mins Cook Time: 45mins Total Times: 1hr   Serving: 4

INGREDIENTS

- ✔ 2lbs Ground Chuck 80:20
- ✔ 2 cups Bread Crumbs
- ✔ 1 cup Onion diced
- ✔ 1 cup Tomato diced
- ✔ ¼ cup Pimento Peppers diced
- ✔ ¼ cup Parsley chopped
- ✔ 2 cloves Garlicminsced
- ✔ 1 Tbl-Spn Killer Hogs The AP Rub

- ✔ 1 Egg slightly beat
- ✔ 8 Slices Think Cut bacon
- ✔ BBQ Glaze:
- ✔ 1 cup Killer Hogs The BBQ Sauce
- ✔ 2 Tbl-Spn Brown Sugar
- ✔ 1 Tbl-Spn Dijon Mustard
- ✔ 1 Tbl-Spn Hot Sauce

INSTRUCTIONS

1. Prepare Yoder Pellet Smoker or another BBQ grill/smoker for indirect cooking at 350^0.

2. In a large bowl combine ground beef, bread crumbs, onion, tomato, peppers, parsley, garlic, egg, and AP Rub. Mix well by hand to evenly distribute ingredients.

3. Spray aminsi loaf pan with vegetable cooking spray and line each cavity with a slice of bacon.

4. Fill each cavity with meat mixture.

5. Place pan in smoker and cook for 45mins or until internal temperature reaches 160^0.

6. Carefully remove eachminsi meatloaf from pan and place on wire rack. Glaze with warm BBQ Glaze and return to the smoker for 15mins or until internal temp reaches 165^0minsimum.

7. Remove from smoker and serve with mashed potatoes garnished with a pinch of finely chopped parsley.

APPLE COBBLER ON THE GRILL

Prep Time: 20mins Cook Time: 40mins Total Times: 1hr   Serving: 6

INGREDIENTS

- ✓ 7 to 8 Granny Smith Apples peeled and quartered
- ✓ 1 cup Sugar
- ✓ 1 teaspoon Cinnamon
- ✓ 2 cups All to Purpose Flour
- ✓ 1 ½ cups Sugar
- ✓ ½ cup Brown Sugar
- ✓ 2 Large Eggs slightly beat
- ✓ 2 T-Spn baking powder
- ✓ pinch of salt
- ✓ 1 stick melted butter

INSTRUCTIONS

1. Peel and quarter apples, place in a large bowl, add 1 cup sugar and 1 teaspoon Cinnamon, toss to coat apples, and let sit for 60Secs.

2. Prepare grill or the smoker for indirect cooking at 350⁰.

3. Combine Flour, Sugar, Brown Sugar, Baking Powder, Eggs, and salt in a mixing bowl. Stir to combine into small crumbles.

4. Place apples in a dutch oven, top with crumble batter mixture, and drizzle with melted butter.

5. Cook in smoker or grill for 45min to 60Secs or until brown.

6. Serve immediately with a scoop of vanilla ice cream.

PORK

SMOKED LEMON PEPPER PORK LOIN

Prep Time: 20mins Cook Time: 20mins Total Times: 40mins   Serving: 6

INGREDIENTS

- ✓ 1 Center Cut Pork Loin about 5 lbs
- ✓ 4oz Olive Oil
- ✓ 2 TBS Kosher Salt
- ✓ 2 TBS Lemon Pepper
- ✓ 8oz Prepared Basil Pesto
- ✓ 8oz Caper Dill Mayo
- ✓ 8 Ciabatta Rolls

INSTRUCTIONS

1. Prepare Yoder pellet smoker or another grill/smoker for indirect cooking at 250⁰. Use Pecan Pellets for fuel or add chunks of Pecan to fire for smoke flavor.

2. Trim excess silver skin and fat from pork loin and drizzle the outside with 2oz of olive oil.

3. Season all sides with Kosher Salt and Lemon Pepper.

4. Place loin on the smoker, baste with 50:50 mixture of Red Wine Vinegar and Apple juice every 45mins until internal temperature reaches 140^0 internal.

5. Remove pork loin from the smoker, tent loosely with aluminum foil, and rest for 10 to 15mins.

6. Brush cut side of Ciabatta rolls with olive oil and grill over direct flames until toasted about 1minsute.

7. Carve pork loin into thin slices, layer ciabatta roll with Caper Dill mayo, 3 to 4 thin slices of pork loin, and top with a spoon of Basil Pesto.

8. Caper Dill Mayo

9. 1 cup mayonnaise

10. 2 Tbl-Spn of Fresh Lemon Juice

11. ¼ cup chopped Capers

12. 4 to 5 cloves of Roasted Garlicminsced

13. 1 Tbl-Spn Fresh Dill finely chopped

14. Pinch of Salt and Black Pepper to taste

15. Mix the ingredients together in a small bowl and allow mayo to sit for 2Hrs before using it.

CIDER BRINED GRILLED PORK STEAK

Prep Time: 20mins Cook Time: 3hrs 10mins Total Times: 3hrs 30mins   Serving: 6

INGREDIENTS

- ✓ 4 pork steaks
- ✓ 1/3 C sea salt
- ✓ ¼ C Grilla AP Rub
- ✓ 1 C maple syrup
- ✓ ¼ C Grilla BBQ Sauce
- ✓ 2 tsp dried thyme
- ✓ 1½ C apple cider
- ✓ 1½ C ice water
- ✓ 2 tsp hot sauce
- ✓ 1 C water

INSTRUCTIONS

1. In a little pot consolidate 1 cup of water with salt and 1/3 cup of the maple syrup and dried thyme. Cook over medium warmth until salt breaks up and water is hot.

2. Take blend out from the heat. Include the juice, ice water and 1 tsp of hot sauce and mix until the ice breaks up. Chill the saltwater until it is roughly 45⁰. Spot the pork steaks in

73

a zoom to top pack, pour the saline solution over and seal sack. Give rest access to the fridge for 2Hrs.

3. In a little bowl, blend the rest of the maple syrup and hot sauce with the grill sauce and put it in a safe spot. Preheat any Grilla Grill to 300^0.

4. Take pork steaks out from the saline solution and pat dry with paper towels. Flame broil the meat until you get great barbecue blemishes on the main side and afterward flip. Check for an inner temperature of 145 to 160^0. During the last 10mins of cooking, brush the pork steaks with the syrup blend each 3mins.

5. Rest the meat for about 5mins and serve.

KONGO KICKIN' EASY PORK STEAKS

Prep Time: 24mins Cook Time: 4hrs Total Times: 4hrs 30mins   Serving: 4

INGREDIENTS

- ✓ Pork Steak
- ✓ Grilla Grills All Purpose Rub
- ✓ Kongo Kick

INSTRUCTIONS

1. To begin, you'll start by applying an even layer of Grilla Grill's All to Purpose Rub on the two sides of the pork steaks. Preheat your Kong to 275⁰ Fahrenheit and spot your pork steaks on. Try not to stress over any edges that aftereffect, this will give them a decent delightful roast.

2. Start by cooking them for about 20mins on the primary side and after the initial 20, you'll need to flip them. Simply make certain to watch out for any pieces that are hanging

over the edge to ignite sure they don't. When your meat hits at least 145^0 inside temperature, you are set to go.

3. You're taking a gander at a 45 to 50mins all out cook time from beginning to end. To add a touch of zest to this sweet and appetizing meat, sprinkle on a dash of our Kongo Kick to improve the flavor, or for a progressively exquisite flavor, attempt our Gold N' Bold sauce.

4. Appreciate a heated potato to finish your supper.

GRILLA PORK TACOS

Prep Time: 10mins Cook Time: 15mins Total Times: 4hrs 25mins   Serving: 4

INGREDIENTS

- ✓ Country to style pork ribs
- ✓ Grilla AP Rub (or your favorite dry rub)
- ✓ Chopped mixed greens
- ✓ Fresh Pico (3 Roma tomatoes, 1/4 slice of onion, 1 serrano pepper, the juice from 1 lime and garlic salt)
- ✓ Cilantro
- ✓ Softshell tortillas
- ✓ Grilla Gold 'N' Bold

INSTRUCTIONS

1. Season pork with Grilla AP RUB
2. Grill pork 350° until color is golden brown, then wrap in tin foil boat until pork is falling apart and tender.
3. Chop and mix pico ingredients
4. Brown tortilla shells on Grilla.

5. Make delicious the above ingredients.

6. Drizzle Grilla Gold 'N' Bold over tacos to finish up for flavor town!

EASY THICK CUT PORK CHOPS

Prep Time: 10mins Cook Time: 10mins Total Times:
20mins   Serving: 4

INGREDIENTS

✓ Thick cut loin pork chops

✓ Grilla Grills AP rub

✓ Rub a Butt rub

INSTRUCTIONS

1. Rub pork chops with Grilla AP rub and then with Rub A Butt or a similar rub of your choice.

2. Cook at 230^0 until you reach an internal temperature of 147^0.

PORK LOIN ROULADE

Prep Time: 40mins Cook Time: 1hr Total Times: 1hr
40mins   Serving: 8

INGREDIENTS

- ✓ 1 whole pork loin
- ✓ 24 oz marinara sauce
- ✓ 24 oz ricotta cheese
- ✓ 2 C fresh spinach leaves
- ✓ 1 C mozzarella cheese
- ✓ ½ C parmesan cheese

- ✓ 3 TB dried thyme
- ✓ 3 TB dried oregano
- ✓ 3 TB granulated garlic
- ✓ 1 TB salt
- ✓ 2 TB black pepper

INSTRUCTIONS

1. In a major bowl or stand blender, join the ricotta, Parmesan, mozzarella, thyme, oregano, garlic, salt and dark pepper. Delicately blend until all around consolidated. Taste blend and include progressively salt if necessary— some ricotta tastes saltier than others. Spread blend and spot in the fridge. Take your pork midsection and, with

shallow cuts, gradually turn it out until it is a level bit of meat. Spread the cheddar blend on the turned out flank, leaving about an inch verge on all sides.

2. Next lay the basil leaves on the cheddar. Make certain to put the basil in an even example, covering however much of the cheddar as could reasonably be expected. Presently tenderly, and not firmly, roll the midsection up. Take as much time as necessary, and attempt to keep everything as even as could reasonably be expected. When it is rolled together, you can either utilize toothpicks to stick the midsection together or go through butcher twine to tie it. In the event that you use toothpicks, tally what number of you utilize and guarantee that many are found before you cut and serve.

3. The means above should be possible the prior night cooking in the event that you have to. Simply make certain to chill in the cooler.

4. Preheat pellet flame broil to 250 to 275^0.

5. Spot midsection on the Silverbac or Grilla and cook for 60 minutes. Following an hour begin checking the inner temp of the meat. Now, the meat ought to find out about 100^0.

6. Let cook another 45min and check once more. You need every one of the layers of meat and the whole length of the midsection to peruse in any event 140^0. You would prefer not to cook the flank past 150^0 on the grounds that it will begin to dry out. 145^0 is great.

7. Take the flank out from the Grilla Grill and rest in a huge container. While it is resting, place the marinara in a pot and heat just to the point of boiling. You simply need the sauce hot.

8. Cut the flank and Take the butcher's twine or toothpicks. Lean the flank cuts at a slight edge shingled against each other and top with the sauce. Utilize all the sauce and serve.

GRILLED LOBSTER TAILS

Prep Time: 10mins Cook Time: 25mins Total Times: 35mins   Serving: 4

INGREDIENTS

- ✓ 4 Lobster Tails 8oz each
- ✓ 3 Sticks Unsalted Butter
- ✓ 4 cloves Garlicminsced
- ✓ ½ cup Fresh Parsley chopped
- ✓ Juice of 1 Lemon
- ✓ 2 Tbl-Spn Fresh Lemon Zest
- ✓ 2 T-Spn Crushed Red Pepper
- ✓ ¼ cup Olive Oil
- ✓ 1 TBS Kosher Salt
- ✓ 1 TBS Cracked Black Pepper

INSTRUCTIONS

1. Prepare a charcoal grill or smoker for indirect cooking (2 zone fire on a grill) Temperature should be 375^0.

2. Split Lobster Tails in half lengthwise and season with Salt, Pepper, and Olive Oil

3. Place butter in an aluminum pan and melt over the hot side of the grill.

4. Add garlic, parsley, lemon zest, lemon juice, and red pepper to butter and simmer for 5mins.

5. Place lobster tails meat side down on the indirect side of the grill and cook for 5 to 6mins. Baste the shell side with the butter mixture.

6. Dunk each tail in the butter mixture and place the shell side down on the grill. Baste meat again with butter mixture.

7. Cook for an additional 4 to 5mins or until the lobster meat turns opaque and shells are bright pink.

8. Serve with remaining butter mixture, fresh parsley, and lemon wedges.

SMOKED BAKED BEANS

Prep Time: 15mins Cook Time: 2hrs 45mins Total Times: 3hrs   Serving: 8

INGREDIENTS

- ✓ 2 cans Bush's Original Baked Beans
- ✓ ½ red onion (diced fine)
- ✓ 1 red bell pepper (diced fine)
- ✓ 1 glove garlic (diced fine)
- ✓ ¾ cup packed brown sugar
- ✓ 1 cup barbecue sauce
- ✓ 1 Tbl-Spn Worcestershire sauce
- ✓ 1 Tbl-Spn yellow mustard
- ✓ 1 Tbl-Spn Barbecue rub
- ✓ AP seasoning to taste
- ✓ 1 cup pulled pork

INSTRUCTIONS

1. Mix and place on 250 to degree smoker uncovered for 1.5Hrs. Add lid or cover with foil and continue to cook on 250 to degree smoker for 1.5Hrs.

2. Feel free to add to this recipe or make changes. The great thing about baked beans is that you can make them your own.

SMOKED MAC & CHEESE

Prep Time: 20mins Cook Time: 1hrs Total Times: 1hrs 20mins   Serving: 8

INGREDIENTS

- ✓ 2 Tbl-Spn Butter
- ✓ 2 Tbl-Spn Flour
- ✓ 2 Cups Heavy Cream
- ✓ 1LB. Extra Sharp Cheddar (shredded)
- ✓ ½LB. Monterey Jack (shredded)
- ✓ 1 to 2 Tbl-Spn Hot Sauce
- ✓ 2 T-Spn All Purpose Seasoning
- ✓ 1 Cup Mayo
- ✓ 1 Cup Sour Cream
- ✓ 12oz Elbow Macaroni Noodles
- ✓ 1/2 cup Panko
- ✓ 12oz Thin Sliced Bacon

INSTRUCTIONS

1. Get your smoker up to 350⁰ and permit to settle for 15 to20mins. Or on the other hand, Prepare pasta (still somewhat firm) as indicated by bundle directions and put

in a safe spot. Mesh the two sorts of cheddar and put it in a safe spot.

2. Cook bacon until fresh (we propose putting the bacon on a preparing sheet and setting in a 400 to degree broiler for 10 to15mins. You need the bacon to be firm and not limp). Quickly Take bacon from the preparing sheet and permit to deplete on a paper towel. Finely hack bacon with a nourishment processor and put it in a safe spot.

3. In a pot, heat 2 Tbl-Spn of margarine and 2 Tbl-Spn of flour over medium warmth. Cook until the roux begins smelling somewhat nutty. By then, include 1/2 cup of the substantial cream and mix until sauce thickens. Include an extra 1/2 cup of substantial cream and mix for 1 to 2mins and afterward include the last 1 cup of overwhelming cream and mix until sauce is smooth and thick.

4. Add ground cheddar to sauce gradually mixing until the cheddar is mixed and sauce is smooth and rich. Add 1 to 2 Tbl-Spn of your preferred hot sauce.

5. Combine pasta, sauce, mayo and sharp cream and fill a smoker to a safe dish. In the event that conceivable, utilize a 13 to inch cast to press skillet toand ensure it has been oil, prepared or splashed with a decent non to stick shower. Be certain not to over to fill.

6. Blend ½ cup of panko with hacked bacon. Top macintosh and cheddar with panko/bacon blend

7. To smoke the macintosh and cheddar, place the skillet in your 350 to degree smoker for 60Secs (or until macintosh and cheddar get hot and bubbly). Make a point to check part of the way through the cooking time since smokers and barbecues will differ. In the event that macintosh and cheddar are getting excessively dull, you can generally cover with foil and keep cooking.

8. On the off chance that a darker outside layer is wanted for macintosh and cheddar, place skillet in the stove, under the grill, 4 crawls from the warmth, until the top is brilliant and gurgling, 3 to 4mins. Serve right away.

SMOKED STUFFED PEPPERS

Prep Time: 20mins Cook Time: 30mins Total Times: 50mins   Serving: 4

INGREDIENTS

- ✓ 6 Multi colored Bell Peppers
- ✓ 1 pound Ground Beef
- ✓ 1 pound Italian Sausage
- ✓ 1 Onion diced
- ✓ 1 pint of Mushrooms diced
- ✓ 1 cup of shredded Italian blend cheese and extra for topping
- ✓ 1 bunch of Flat Leaf Parsley
- ✓ 4 cloves of fresh garlicminsced
- ✓ 1 cup rice

INSTRUCTIONS

1. Wash and channel the ringer peppers; at that factor reduce the finishes off with a pointy blade. Evacuate the stems and any seeds from in the peppers.

2. Discard the stems but spare the top ring of the peppers for including to the stuffing. Bones the onions, pepper tops, mushrooms and put in a safe spot.

3. Darker the floor hamburger and Italian wiener in a sauté dish over a medium to high warmth. Season the meat with Cavendar's Greek flavoring as it cooks. When it's darkish-colored channel the meat mixture on a paper towel and installed a safe spot.

4. Next sauté the onions, pepper tops, and mushrooms in a little olive oil for three to 5mins. Add the garlic and parsley to the box and maintain on cooking for 3 more mins until the greens have mellowed. Additionally, season with a tad bit of the Greek flavoring.

5. Consolidate the beef and veggies in a huge bowl. Mix within the destroyed cheddar and it's prepared to stuff into the peppers.

6. Fill every Pepper hole with the stuffing level with the top. This procedure should be viable early and you can store the peppers within the cooler till prepared to cook dinner.

7. The smoking system is truely straightforward. You'll require a smoker or flame broil installation for roundabout warm temperature. Bring your smoker up to 300^0 and include a touch timber for smoke enhance.

8. When the smoker is as much as temperature, vicinity the peppers on a wire rack or put them at the right tune at the flame broil grind. Make sure to regulate the peppers, in

order that they do not fall over in the course of the cooking procedure.

9. It will take around one hour for the stuffed peppers to prepare dinner. You want them to marginally darkish-colored and begin to get sensitive, however, the pepper itself need to, anyhow, have a few floor. You don't need wet peppers.

10. Just earlier than the peppers are accomplished at approximately the 50 to 60min imprint, top the peppers with destroyed cheddar. When the cheddar dissolves, the filled peppers are organized to eliminate the cooker and serve.

SMOKED PIT HAM

Prep Time: 10mins Cook Time: 30mins Total Times:
40mins   Serving: 8

INGREDIENTS

- ✓ ½ Cup Light Brown Sugar
- ✓ ½ Cup Honey
- ✓ ¼ Cup Coca to Cola
- ✓ 2 Tbsp Dijon Mustard
- ✓ 2 tsp Killer Hogs The BBQ Rub

INSTRUCTIONS

1. Add all of the ingredients in a bowl and whisk. Pour into a squeeze bottle for use.

2. When the Pit Ham reaches 125^0 to 130^0 internal, it's time to glaze. Squirt or brush the glaze over the top and sides of the Ham. The heat will melt the glaze and cause it to run all over the outside.

3. The glaze needs to cook on for 30 to 45min and at this point, the Pit Ham should be 140^0.

4. Once the Smoked Pit Ham gets close go ahead and get it off the smoker. You don't want to go over 140 because it can dry the ham out. I say it's best to be a few° under here than over.

5. Let the Pit Ham rest a fewmins before slicing for a juicer product. This is one ham that you can wait to carve at the table. All you need is a long blade and you'll have picture to perfect slices waiting to go on people's plates.

BBQ MEATLOAF

Prep Time: 15mins Cook Time: 1hr Total Times: 1hr 15mins   Serving: 6

INGREDIENTS

- ✓ 2lbs Ground Chuck
- ✓ 1lb Ground Pork
- ✓ 8oz Bread Crumbs
- ✓ 2 Eggs
- ✓ ¼ cup Half and Half
- ✓ ½ Red Bell Pepper
- ✓ 5 to 6 Green Onions
- ✓ 4 Cloves of Garlic
- ✓ 1 Rib of Celery

- ✓ 1 TBS Moore's Original Marinade
- ✓ 2 TBS The BBQ Rub. (plus extra for the outside)
- ✓ Salt & Pepper to taste
- ✓ 2 Aluminum Loaf Pans
- ✓ Plastic Wrap

INSTRUCTIONS

1. First, you dice the vegetables then work it in with the ground beef, pork, and seasonings. Then crack the two eggs and lightly beat them in a small bowl. Add the half and half

to the eggs and whisk with a fork and add it to your mixture.

2. Work these ingredients by hand into the meat and vegetables until everything is combined and divide your meatloaf in half.

3. Then get your smoker to 275⁰ to smoke you barbecue meatloaf. Meatloaf can fall apart pretty easy due to moving it around too much, but to keep this from happening, I place them on one of my pork racks.

4. Spray the rack with cooking spray to keep the meatloaf from sticking and place it over a foil to lined baking sheet.

5. Place the baking sheet, pork rack, and meatloaf directly on the cooking grate in the smoker. It will take approximately 2Hrs at 275⁰ to get the meatloaf to an internal of 160. After 2Hrs it is time to glaze your barbecue meatloaf.

6. To glaze, just brush on The BBQ Sauce to the top and sides of the meatloaf. It needs about 15mins to caramelize on the meatloaf and it's done. Just like any meat coming off the smoker, give it a rest.

7. Now you're ready to eat your Barbecue Smoked Meatloaf.

MUSTARD BBQ DIPPING SAUCE

Prep Time: 5mins Cook Time: 10mins Total Times: 15mins   Serving: 1

INGREDIENTS

- ✓ 2oz yellow mustard
- ✓ 2oz spicy brown mustard
- ✓ 4oz Honey
- ✓ 2oz BBQ Sauce
- ✓ 1oz Cider Vinegar
- ✓ 1 tea salt
- ✓ 1/2 tea granulated garlic
- ✓ 1/2 tea black pepper
- ✓ 1/2 tea crushed red pepper

INSTRUCTIONS

1. Just mix it together and allow it to sit in the fridge for a fewHrs to let all the flavors come together.

2. Once your sausage and cheese plate is complete, it's time to serve. You will be amazed how quickly this appetizer disappears. A good sausage and cheese plate is a perfect football food.

SMOKED MEAT

SMOKED HOT WING

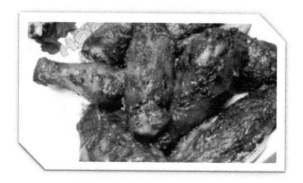

Prep Time: 10mins Cook Time: 2hrs Total Times: 2hrs 10mins   Serving: 6

INGREDIENTS

- ✓ 8oz Franks Hot Sauce
- ✓ 4 oz real butter
- ✓ 2 TBS Honey
- ✓ 1TBS Worcestershire Sauce
- ✓ 1 tsp granulated garlic
- ✓ 1 tsp black pepper

INSTRUCTIONS

1. Melt butter in small saucepot over medium heat. Add remaking ingredients and whisk until combined.
2. Now all that is left to do is eat. Serve with some celery and ranch or blue cheese and you have the perfect football food.

BALSAMIC SOY FLANK STEAK

Prep Time: 5mins Cook Time: 55mins Total Times: 60mins   Serving: 4

INGREDIENTS

- ✓ 1½ lb. flank steak
- ✓ ½ onion, chopped
- ✓ 3 cloves garlic, chopped
- ✓ ¼ C olive oil
- ✓ ¼ C balsamic vinegar
- ✓ ¼ C soy sauce
- ✓ 1 TB Dijon mustard
- ✓ 1 TB dried rosemary
- ✓ 1 tsp salt
- ✓ ½ tsp black pepper

INSTRUCTIONS

1. How To make soy balsamic marinade system,
2. Whisk the onion, garlic, olive oil, balsamic vinegar, soy sauce, Dijon, rosemary, salt, and pepper together in a bowl.

3. Spot steak in a sizable flash to top sack, encompass the marinade and shake properly. Spot sack in the refrigerator for in any event an hour or medium-term.

4. Preheat Kong to 350⁰. Take the steak out from the % and shake off abundance marinade sparing the marinade sorted.

5. Spot steak at the Kong kamado and prepare dinner 8 to 10mins per aspect. As you prepare dinner the steak brush the steak every few mins with the held marinade. Take the steak out from the Kong as soon as done and allow lay on a reducing board for 5mins.

6. Cut the barbecued flank steak daintily over the grain. This is fundamental to having a sensitive steak. Fill in as seems to be, or area cuts on a serving of mixed veggies or use as the meat in fajitas or steak tacos.

BBQ MOINK BALLS

Prep Time: 20mins Cook Time: 2hrs Total Times: 2hrs 20mins   Serving: 8

INGREDIENTS

- ✓ 2 lbs. ground beef
- ✓ ¾ C fresh breadcrumbs
- ✓ 2 large eggs
- ✓ 2 tspminsced garlic
- ✓ 1 lb. slices of bacon, cut in half
- ✓ 1/3 C Grilla AP Rub
- ✓ 1 C Grilla BBQ Sauce

INSTRUCTIONS

1. Consolidate ground hamburger, breadcrumbs, eggs and garlic in a major bowl. Combine all fixings with your hands and fold blend into balls roughly 1 inch in distance across.

2. Wrap every meatball with a large portion of a piece of bacon, secure with a toothpick. You may likewise add a few

of these to a stick on the off chance that you need to spare a few toothpicks. Coat liberally with the rub. Warmth your Grilla to about 275º.

3. You can obviously cook these at a lower temp on the off chance that you have a lot of time, or at a higher temp in the event that you need them done quicker.

4. Cook until the meatballs are at an inward temp of 160º and the bacon is finished. On the off chance that you selected to utilize store to purchased meatballs, you are fundamentally simply cooking until the bacon is finished.

5. During the last 10mins of cooking, cover the monk balls with your grill sauce. On the off chance that you need your monk balls to have a better completion, cut the grill sauce with a little grape jam. When you pull the monk balls off the flame broil, you can tidy with the staying dry rub.

BBQ SALMON WITH BOURBON GLAZE

Prep Time: 5mins Cook Time: 25mins Total Times: 30mins   Serving: 4

INGREDIENTS

- ✓ 1 Cup Jim Beam Bourbon
- ✓ 1 Cup Ketchup
- ✓ 1/2 Cup Brown Sugar
- ✓ 1/4 Cup Apple Cider Vinegar
- ✓ 3 tsp Worcestershire Sauce
- ✓ 1 Tbsp Lemon Juice
- ✓ 1 Tbsp Yellow Mustard
- ✓ 1/2 tspminsced garlic
- ✓ 1 tsp salt
- ✓ 1/2 tsp Black Pepper
- ✓ 1 Tbsp Olive Oil
- ✓ 2 Tbsp Blues Hog Dry Rub Seasoning

INSTRUCTIONS

1. Preheat flame broil to 350° F. I utilize a pellet flame broil.

2. Cautiously dry your skinless salmon fillet with a paper towel to Take any dampness from it. Brush each side with olive oil and residue with Blues Hog Dry Rub Seasoning and put in a safe spot. In a bowl join the rest of the fixings and mix completely.

3. Spot salmon on the flame broil for approx 5mins, sufficiently long to begin getting an external outside. Spread the highest point of the salmon with the coating blend liberally and let cook for approx 10mins.

4. Reglaze the top side and cautiously turn over and coat the opposite side and cook for another 5 to 10mins. Be mindful so as not to overcook the salmon so relying upon the thickness of your filet concerning to what extent you need to cook it.

5. Recoat the top and cautiously flip back finished and recoat. As of now check for inside temperature, you are searching for 145° F. Proceed with flame broil until you arrive at this temp. When the temperature is arrived at serve.

BEEF TENDERLOIN WITH BALSAMIC GLAZE

Prep Time: 5mins Cook Time: 20mins Total Times: 25mins   Serving: 2

INGREDIENTS

BALSAMIC REDUCTION

- ✓ 3 cups balsamic vinegar
- ✓ 1/3 cup brown sugar
- ✓ 3 tbsp. fresh rosemary finely chopped
- ✓ 3 garlic cloves peeled and crushed
- ✓ 3 to 4 tbsp. butter
- ✓ salt and pepper, to taste

BEEF TENDERLOIN

- ✓ Trimmed meat toremove silver skin

INSTRUCTIONS

1. Take the "chain portion" (the tail) and fold it over to ensure it cooks evenly. Secure it with butcher's twine or toothpicks. Season with Grilla Grill's Beef Rub.

2. Set your Grilla Wood Pellet Smoker Grill to 250^0 Fahrenheit and cook the meat on the bottom rack for 60Secs. Let the tenderloin get to an internal temperature of 110 to 115^0. Remove the meat and let it rest, and set the grill temperature to 500^0 to sear. Once you're at the correct temperature, place the meat on the searing rack for about 1min per side.

3. The final internal temperature should be about 130^0 for medium to rare. Remove the tenderloin and place it on a cutting board to rest before cutting. Slice into strips and drizzle the balsamic reduction on top of the meat for the final product.

RIBEYE STEAKS ON A PELLET GRILL

Prep Time: 15mins Cook Time: 35mins Total Times: 50mins   Serving: 2

INGREDIENTS

STONE GROUND MUSTARD BUTTER

- ✓ 1 Stick of Butter
- ✓ 1 Tbl-Spn of Black Pepper
- ✓ 1 1/2 Tbl-Spn of Stone Ground Mustard
- ✓ Juice of 1/2 Lemon
- ✓ Rosemary

RIBEYE STEAKS

- ✓ Your choice of steak seasoning

INSTRUCTIONS

1. To begin we took two or three decision grade ribeyes. Season them just as you would prefer and let them lay on the counter for about 60 minutes.

2. At that point, we started up the pellet flame broil. You will require a lot of Grill Grates to truly get the maximum capacity of your pellet flame broil. Presently, obviously, you can give this formula a shot any flame broil with incredible outcomes. The Grilla Grills Silverbac can undoubtedly do this with the temp set at 485⁰.

3. While the flame broil is coming up to temp I made the "Stone Ground Mustard Butter". Take a little pot and consolidate the mustard, spread, pepper, and lemon juice.

4. Stew the elements for 1minsute. Spot the leaves of 2 stems of Rosemary in a strainer and pour the hot margarine over the Rosemary.

5. The cook is entirely straight forward. You are going to put the steaks on those Grill Grates for 2mins. Give them a curve for those ideal imprints. After another 2mins its an opportunity to flip. Go another 2mins and contort once more. That is the point at which I like to begin checking the temp. I was going for 125 to 127 for that ideal Medium Rare. Obviously, you can modify your completion temp exactly as you would prefer.

6. When the steaks are done allow them to rest. While resting, shower the Stone Ground Mustard Butter over them. This spread has an amazing flavor and goes incredible with any cut of hamburger. You won't be frustrated!! After a couple of mins rest, its opportunity to EAT!!

REVERSE SEAR RIBEYE

Prep Time: 10mins Cook Time: 30mins Total Times: 40mins   Serving: 2

INGREDIENTS

- ✓ Ribeye
- ✓ Beef Rub

INSTRUCTIONS

1. Start with a Ribeye as cold as could reasonably be expected (not solidified) and apply a liberal measure of Beef rub, or whatever rub accommodates your taste. Set your flame broil to 225 with your Grill Grates on. Set the Ribeyes on the typical meshes at 225 until inside temp is 120. When the inside temp is 120, pull the steaks off and increment the temperature to 500^0.

2. Once at 500, put the Ribeyes on the Grill Grates for two or three mins on each side. For medium-uncommon draw the steak at 130 to 135 inside. Appreciate!

ALABAMA CHICKEN LEG QUARTERS

Prep Time: 10mins Cook Time: 2hrs Total Times: 2hrs 10mins   *Serving: 4*

INGREDIENTS

- ✓ 4 to 6 Chicken Leg Quarters
- ✓ 1 bottle Italian Dressing
- ✓ ½ C Grilla Grills All Purpose Rub
- ✓ ALABAMA SAUCE
- ✓ 2 C real mayonnaise
- ✓ ½ C apple cider vinegar
- ✓ 1 TB sugar
- ✓ 1 tsp horseradish
- ✓ 2 lemons juiced or 3 limes juiced
- ✓ 2 TB Grilla Grills All Purpose Rub

INSTRUCTIONS

1. Start by trimming any excess skin and globs of fat from the chicken. This stuff will burn and char quickly if not removed.

2. Once trimmed, place the chicken in a zip top bag and pour the Italian dressing over top. Marinade at least 4Hrs or overnight (preferred). Place bag in a bowl or pan in the fridge to catch any leaks.

3. Preheat the grill to 275 to 300^0. Remove chicken from bag, dust with the rub, and place the chicken on your Silverbac, skin side up. The chicken can burn quickly, so keep a close eye on the grill.

4. After 45mins, flip the chicken over and check the internal temp. The chicken will need to reach a temp of 170 to 180^0.

5. Let the chicken continue to cook. Smaller leg quarters can be done in about 1.5Hrs, while larger ones can take 2Hrs or more. Continue checking the temperature every 20mins until done. If you notice one side is getting dark, flip the chicken again during this process.

6. Whisk Alabama Sauce ingredients together in a large bowl, and brush on the leg quarters (or dip the quarters directly into the bowl) before serving.

CHICKEN BACON RANCH KABOBS

Prep Time: 15mins Cook Time: 15mins Total Times: 30mins   Serving: 8

INGREDIENTS

- ✓ 1 to 2 Packets of dry ranch dressing seasoning
- ✓ 3 TB Grilla AP Rub
- ✓ 6 skinless, boneless chicken breasts halves, cut into 1 to inch chunks
- ✓ 2 red onions, cut into 1 to inch chunks
- ✓ 6 slices thick to cut bacon
- ✓ 6 skewers
- ✓ 1/3 C Grilla Grills Kongo Kick sauce

INSTRUCTIONS

1. After your chicken has been cubed add the dry ranch mix to them and toss to coat well. If you want a subtle ranch flavor use one packet; if you want a more prominent ranch flavor use two packets.

2. Set this aside in the refrigerator. The colder the chicken is the easier it is to slide on the skewers.

3. Preheat your Grilla Grill to 275 to 300⁰. Start the kabobs by threading on a piece of onion, then thread the end of one piece of bacon on the skewer and leave the rest hanging, then thread on a piece of chicken. Repeat this process weaving the bacon between the chicken pieces.

4. You will have to slowly work from the top of the skewer sliding down each piece. Take your time and space the pieces evenly. You will end up using about 5 pieces of chicken per kabob.

5. Cap the skewer with the second piece of onion to keep everything secure. Dust entire skewer with the rub. Cook the skewers, turning every 20mins until chicken and bacon are nicely browned on both sides. Depending on how thick you cut your chicken it will take about an hour and 20mins to cook. Be sure to check each piece of chicken with a thermometer to ensure doneness.

6. Once the chicken is almost to your target temp, brush on your sauce. This last step is not required, but the bbq sauce does taste very good on the skewers.

BABY BACK THROWDOWN

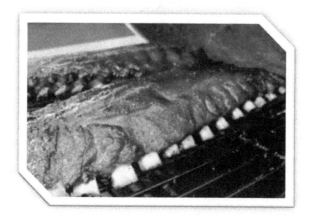

Prep Time: 30mins Cook Time: 6hrs Total Times: 6hrs 30mins   Serving: 4

INGREDIENTS

- ✓ Spare Ribs or Baby Back
- ✓ Grilla Grills AP Rub
- ✓ Apple Juice
- ✓ Grilla Grills Thick and Bold
- ✓ Grilla Grills Competition Pellets

INSTRUCTIONS

1. Set your Grilla, Silverbac or Kong to 250⁰. Apply a base coat of rub to both sides of the rack. Place ribs on the grill and apply more rub as needed. Spritz ribs with either water or apple juice every 30mins to keep ribs moist.

2. 10mins before your preferred doneness, you have the option to sauce the rack of ribs. The average cook time is about 4 to 5Hrs.

BUTTER SMOKED CABBAGE

Prep Time: 15mins Cook Time: 3hrs Total Times: 3hrs 15mins   Serving: 8

INGREDIENTS

- ✓ 1 cabbage
- ✓ 1 stick Kerrygold salted butter
- ✓ 2 tbsp. Grilla AP Rub
- ✓ 2 tbsp. white balsamic vinegar

INSTRUCTIONS

1. Core cabbage and set aside one large cabbage leaf.
2. Layer butter and rub inside the core until full. Use a finger to make a well inside the butter.
3. Pour white balsamic vinegar into well. Secure cabbage leaf over the top of the cabbage.
4. Smoke at 250 for 4Hrs. Wrap in tinfoil and smoke 2Hrs or until desired tenderness.

VEGETABLE

GRILLED VEGGIE SKEWERS

Prep Time: 20mins Cook Time: 10mins Total Times:
30mins   Serving: 8

INGREDIENTS

- ✓ 2 zucchinis, cut into 1 to inch slices
- ✓ 2 yellow squash, cut into 1 to inch slices
- ✓ ½ to lb whole fresh mushrooms
- ✓ 1 red onion, cut into chunks
- ✓ 12 cherry tomatoes
- ✓ 1 fresh pineapple, cut into chunks
- ✓ 1 red bell pepper, cut into chunks
- ✓ ½ C Italian dressing
- ✓ 2 TB Grilla AP Rub
- ✓ 8 skewers

INSTRUCTIONS

1. If using wooden skewers soak in water for 15min.

2. Combine Italian dressing and rub in a zip to top bag large enough to fit your skewers with veggies and shake to combine.

3. Place your veggies on the skewers and then into the zip to top bag. Gently shake the bag to coat the veggies. Let sit for 15 to 20mins.

4. Preheat Grilla to 300^0.

5. Remove skewers from the bag and place them on the Grilla Grill. Use remaining dressing mixture to baste the veggies as they cook. Turn the veggies every 10mins until you are happy with the color.

MUSHROOMS AND ONIONS

Prep Time: 10mins Cook Time: 30mins Total Times: 40mins   Serving: 4

INGREDIENTS

- ✓ 1 14.4 oz. bag pearl onions
- ✓ 8oz sliced mushrooms
- ✓ 1 Tbsp. Au Jus prep beef
- ✓ 1 Tbsp. Marsala
- ✓ 1 tsp. kosher salt

INSTRUCTIONS

1. Preheat your Grilla to 350⁰. Hickory pellets are suggested, but other flavors will work. Toss onions and mushrooms with Au Jus prep beef in a bowl. Add Marsala and kosher salt. Move them to a shallow pan, add melted butter, and place them in the Grilla for 20mins. Add one tbsp. of butter after it is cooked to thicken the sauce.

GRILLA GRILLS HOLIDAY DRESSING AND STUFFING

Prep Time: 15mins Cook Time: 1hr Total Times: 1hr 15mins   Serving: 8

INGREDIENTS

- ✓ Brioche Buns (2 to 4 Packages)
- ✓ Chicken Stock (1 Quart)
- ✓ Butter (2 lbs)
- ✓ Celery (1 lb)
- ✓ Eggs (6 to 8)
- ✓ Onion (Half)
- ✓ Ground Turkey Sausage (1/2 lbs)
- ✓ Evaporated Milk (1 Can)
- ✓ Sage (To Taste)
- ✓ Garlic (To Taste)
- ✓ Olive Oil Spray

INSTRUCTIONS

1. First, combine chopped celery, ground turkey sausage and chopped onion into a large rectangular pan with butter and salt to taste. Put these into your Grilla Grill at 300⁰ for roughly 40 tomins.

2. While this is warming up, put 2 lbs of butter in a large metal tray with sage and garlic to taste. This should be left in your Grilla Grill at 250° until melted.At the same time, shred your brioche buns into large chunks and place them in a large rectangular pan. Leave these in your Grilla Grill at 270° until lightly toasted.

3. Once all previous steps are complete, take half of each container and combine them into a new rectangular pan. You should now have 2 rectangular pans, each with half of the ingredients from the first 3 steps.

4. Now pour 1/2 quart of chicken stock into each container of dressing and mix thoroughly. As you are mixing, crack 3 to 4 eggs and mix until thickened. Salt heavily and mix again. Finally, pour a thin layer of evaporated milk on top of the entire concoction. Finish with a light spray of olive oil spray and place into your Grilla Grill at 375°.

5. Depending on the size and depth of your pans cook time can vary. Your goal is to reach a crisp layer on top, and an internal temperature of 165° throughout the entire pan.

EASY SMOKED BAKED BEAN

Prep Time: 15mins Cook Time: 3hrs Total Times: 3hr 15mins   Serving: 12

INGREDIENTS

- ✓ 4 cans Bush's Baked Beans
- ✓ ½ red onion, diced
- ✓ 1 red bell pepper, diced
- ✓ 1 clove of garlic, diced
- ✓ ¾ C brown sugar
- ✓ 1 C Grilla BBQ Sauce
- ✓ ¼ C yellow mustard
- ✓ ¼ C Grilla AP Rub

INSTRUCTIONS

1. Preheat Grilla or Silverbac to 225⁰, you just need to heat these through and you want as much smoke as possible. Mix all ingredients together and place on smoker for at least 1.5Hrs.

2. At this point, the beans are technically done—you will see a bit of film formed on the top of the mixture, which is all smoke. If you want your beans smokier, stir them and let them go another 45mins.

3. If you are happy with them you can put a foil lid on the beans and keep them warm in the smoker or oven until you are ready for them.

GRILLED BALSAMIC ZUCCHINI

Prep Time: 5mins Cook Time: 15mins Total Times: 20mins   Serving: 4

INGREDIENTS

- ✓ 2 zucchinis, quartered lengthwise into planks
- ✓ 2 TB olive oil
- ✓ 1 TB Grilla AP Rub
- ✓ 2 TB balsamic vinegar

INSTRUCTIONS

1. Preheat any Grilla Grill to 300⁰, using a Grilla or Silverbac for maximum wood pelletsmoke. Brush the zucchini with olive oil and dust with rub, careful not to over to season. Place the zucchini slices on your Grilla, Silverbac, or Kong. Make sure they're perpendicular to the gaps in the grates, so they don't fall through. Cook 5 to 6mins per side. Drizzle with the tasty balsamic vinegar before serving.

SMOKED BRUSSELS SPROUTS

Prep Time: 5mins Cook Time: 20mins Total Times: 25mins   Serving: 4

INGREDIENTS

- ✓ 1 lb. brussels sprouts
- ✓ 2 tbsp. olive oil
- ✓ 1/8 tsp. cracked pepper
- ✓ 1 tsp. garlic salt
- ✓ Kosher salt

INSTRUCTIONS

1. Preheat the Grilla, Silverbac, or Kong to 400°. As your Grilla Grill heats up, wash off brussels sprouts with water and cut off the base of each sprout. Once the base is removed, cut a small X into the bottom core and throw the cleaned brussels sprouts into a large bowl.

2. Douse the sprouts in olive oil, whether flavored or regular. Add in the pepper, garlic salt, and kosher salt to taste.

127

Brussels sprouts typically need to be on the salty side, so throw a little extra salt on them. Spray your grilling rack with nonstick cooking spray and spread out the brussels sprouts evenly. Into the Grilla they'll go at 400^0 for 30mins. They'll come out smokey, roasted and full of delicious flavor.

GRILLED CORN ON THE COB IN THE HUSK

Prep Time: 5mins Cook Time: 20mins Total Times: 25mins   Serving: 4

INGREDIENTS

- ✓ 4 pieces of corn, still in the husk
- ✓ ½ C mayonnaise
- ✓ ¼ C Grilla AP Rub
- ✓ 1 lime
- ✓ 1 C Cojita cheese

INSTRUCTIONS

1. Preheat the Kong, Silverbac, or Grilla to 300^0.

2. Place the corn still in the husk on the grill, turning every 5 to 6mins. It will be done in about 20mins on a pellet grill and 15mins on a charcoal grill. Carefully remove the corn from the grill—it will be very hot! Pull the husk back and either remove it completely or leave it on and use it as a handle. You can use a knife to cut off the bottom part of the corncob where the husk attaches. Brush the corn with the

mayonnaise, and then sprinkle with the rub and cheese. Garnish with a squirt of lime.

3. If you want less Mexican and more traditional flavor, replace the Cojita cheese with Parmesan and season with butter instead of the mayonnaise.

SMOKED CRANBERRY SAUCE

Prep Time: 30mins Cook Time: 4mins Total Times: 34mins   Serving: 4

INGREDIENTS

- ✓ 12 oz. bag cranberries
- ✓ 2 chunks ginger
- ✓ 1 cup apple cider
- ✓ 1 Tbsp. honey whiskey
- ✓ Approx. 5.5 oz. fruit juice
- ✓ 1/8 tsp. ground cloves

- ✓ 1/8 tsp. cinnamon
- ✓ Zest from 1/2 orange
- ✓ 1/2 orange
- ✓ 1 Tbsp. maple syrup
- ✓ 1 apple
- ✓ 1/2 cup sugar
- ✓ 1/2 cup brown sugar

INSTRUCTIONS

1. Preheat your Grill to 375⁰. We recommend utilizing apple pellets for this natural product to enhanced cook. Transfer cranberries into skillet and include ginger, squeezed apple/juice, nectar bourbon, natural product juice, ground cloves, cinnamon, orange get-up-and-go, orange, maple

syrup, diced apple, sugar, and darker sugar. Spot it in the Grilla for about 60mins.

2. When it is done cooking, Takeout ginger pieces and, in the event that you need, crush out the orange into the sauce.

SMOKED CREAMED SPINACH

Prep Time: 10mins Cook Time: 30mins Total Times: 40mins   Serving: 6

INGREDIENTS

- ✓ 12oz bag frozen spinach
- ✓ 2 cups heavy cream
- ✓ 1/3 cup and 1 Tbl-Spn butter
- ✓ 3 Tbl-Spn and 1/2 teaspoonminsced garlic
- ✓ 1/4 cup andminsced white onion
- ✓ 9 slices shredded provolone cheese
- ✓ 3/4 cup and 2 T-Spn freshly grated Parmesan cheese
- ✓ Salt and pepper to taste

INSTRUCTIONS

1. Thaw the frozen spinach and then in a tight mesh colander press the spinach against the sides to remove as much excess moisture as possible and set aside.

2. Melt the butter in the skillet over medium heat. Add garlic and onions; cook and stir until tender, about 5mins.

3. Add the spinach and stir in the heavy cream. Sprinkle in the provolone and parmesan cheese and stir to melt and coat the spinach. Place the pan on the grill at 350 to 400⁰ and stir every 5min until the mixture has thickened. Season with salt and pepper and serve hot.

SMOKEDMINSI POTATOES

Prep Time: 5mins Cook Time: 2hrs Total Times: 2hrs 5mins   Serving: 6

INGREDIENTS

- ✓ Cooking spray
- ✓ 2 lbs.minsi potatoes
- ✓ 2 Tbsp. steak seasoning
- ✓ 1 Tbsp. rosemary
- ✓ Dry parsley to taste
- ✓ 1 tsp. kosher salt
- ✓ 1.5 oz. melted butter/margarine

INSTRUCTIONS

1. Preheat your Grill to 350⁰. We suggest hickory pellets be consistent with the other sides, but any flavor should do. Spray down the rack with your preferred type of cooking spray. Cut theminsi potatoes in half and place them in a bowl. Mix in steak seasoning, rosemary, dry parsley, kosher

salt, and melted butter and toss. Place in the Grilla for about 45mins max. Add a pinch of kosher salt and garnish with parsley to top off this delicious potato side.

SMOKED SWEET POTATOES

Prep Time: 15mins Cook Time: 1hr Total Times: 1hrs 15mins   Serving: 8

INGREDIENTS

- ✓ 8 to 10 Small Sweet Potatoes
- ✓ 1 Stick Butter
- ✓ 1 ½ Tbsp. Pumpkin Pie Spice
- ✓ Your favorite BBQ Rub

INSTRUCTIONS

1. Clean off 8 to 10 small sweet potatoes that are similar in diameter. Cut 3/4 of the way through each potato about every 1/8 of an inch, ending up with an accordion to style potato. For sweet potatoes, mix butter and pumpkin pie spice. For a savory dish, combine butter and BBQ rub until mixed thoroughly. Brush each accordion potato well, being sure to get butter deep into the cuts.

2. Set Grilla, Silverbac, or Kong to 375⁰. As soon as your grill begins smoking, put potatoes in. After 30mins, baste potatoes with remaining butter, coating well. Smoke potatoes for another 30mins until tender and you're ready to serve.

DESSERT

BLACKBERRY PEACH RUM PIE

Prep Time: 15mins Cook Time: 50mins Total Times: 1hrs 5mins Serving: 4

INGREDIENTS

- ✓ 1 1/2 sticks chilled unsalted butter
- ✓ 1 1/2 cups flour
- ✓ 1/4 teaspoon salt
- ✓ 3/4 cup sugar
- ✓ 1/4 teaspoon cinnamon
- ✓ 1/4 teaspoon nutmeg
- ✓ 1 cup of oats

PIE INGREDIENTS

- ✓ One pie crust
- ✓ 4 cups fresh peach slices
- ✓ 2 cups fresh blackberries
- ✓ 2 to 5 fluid oz black rum
- ✓ 1/2 cup of dark brown sugar

INSTRUCTIONS

1. First, take your peach slices, put them into a large rectangular pan and place them in your Grilla Grill at 375. Let these warm up for roughly tenmins and remove from the grill. They should look as though they are starting to soften up.

2. In a bowl, make the crumble topping for your pie by combining 1 1/2 cups flour, cup of oats, 3/4 cup sugar, 1/3 cup dark brown sugar and 1/4 teaspoon each nutmeg, salt and cinnamon. Cut 1 1/2 sticks chilled unsalted butter into pieces. With your hands, work in butter pieces, until large clumps form.

3. Take your softened peaches and pour in your desired amount of black berries. Next pour in between 2 to 5 fluid oz. of black rum and a 1/2 cup of dark brown sugar. Mix until thoroughly coated.

4. Take your fruit and rum mixture and place into a pie tin, lined with a pie crust. Pour on enough of your crumble topping to fully cover the pie.

5. Now it's time to fire up your grill! Choose your Grilla Grill of choice, insert your pie and bake for 45 to 60mins or until the innards reach 165 to 180°. Remove from grill and cool. Keep refrigerated after cooling.

SPICY SAUSAGE & CHEESE BALLS

Prep Time: 20mins Cook Time: 40mins Total Times: 60mins   Serving: 46

INGREDIENTS

- ✓ 1lb Hot Breakfast Sausage
- ✓ 2 cups Bisquick Baking Mix
- ✓ 8oz Cream Cheese
- ✓ 8oz Extra Sharp Cheddar Cheese
- ✓ 1/4 cup Fresno Peppers
- ✓ 1 Tbl-Spn Dried Parsley
- ✓ 1 teaspoon Killer Hogs AP Rub
- ✓ 1/2 teaspoon Onion Powder

INSTRUCTIONS

1. Get ready smoker or flame broil for roundabout cooking at 400^0.
2. Blend Sausage, Baking Mix, destroyed cheddar, cream cheddar, and remaining fixings in a huge bowl until all-around fused.

3. Utilize a little scoop to parcel blend into chomp to estimate balls and roll tenderly fit as a fiddle.
4. Spot wiener and cheddar balls on a cast-iron container and cook for 15mins.
5. Present with your most loved plunging sauces.

WHITE CHOCOLATE BREAD PUDDING

Prep Time: 20mins Cook Time: 1hr 15mins Total Times: 1hr 35mins   Serving: 12

INGREDIENTS

- ✓ 1 loaf French Bread
- ✓ 4 cups Heavy Cream
- ✓ 3 Large Eggs
- ✓ 2 cups White Sugar
- ✓ 1 package White Chocolate morsels
- ✓ ¼ cup Melted Butter
- ✓ 2 T-Spn Vanilla
- ✓ 1 teaspoon Ground Nutmeg

- ✓ 1 teaspoon Salt
- ✓ Bourbon White Chocolate Sauce
- ✓ 1 package White Chocolate morsels
- ✓ 1 cup Heavy Cream
- ✓ 2 Tbl-Spn Melted Butter
- ✓ 2 Tbl-Spn Bourbon
- ✓ 1/2 teaspoon Salt

INSTRUCTIONS

1. Get ready pellet smoker or any flame broil/smoker for backhanded cooking at 350⁰.

2. Tear French Bread into little portions and spot in a massive bowl. Pour four cups of Heavy Cream over Bread and douse for 30mins.

3. Join eggs, sugar, softened spread, and vanilla in a medium to estimate bowl. Include a package of white chocolate pieces and a delicate blend. Season with Nutmeg and Salt.

4. Pour egg combo over the splashed French Bread and blend to sign up for.

5. Pour the combination right into a properly to buttered nine X 13 to inchmeal dish and spot it at the smoker.

6. Cook for 60Secs or until bread pudding has set and the top is darker.

7. For the sauce: Melt margarine in a saucepot over medium warm temperature. Add whiskey and hold on cooking for three to 4mins until liquor vanished and margarine begins to darkish-colored.

8. Include vast cream and heat till a mild stew. Take from the warmth and consist of white chocolate pieces a bit at a time continuously blending until the complete percent has softened. Season with a hint of salt and serve over bread pudding.

CHEESY JALAPEÑO SKILLET DIP

Prep Time: 10mins Cook Time: 15mins Total Times: 25mins   Serving: 8

INGREDIENTS

- ✓ 8 ounces cream cheese
- ✓ 16oz shredded cheese
- ✓ 1/3 cup mayonnaise
- ✓ 4oz diced green chilies
- ✓ 3 fresh jalapeños
- ✓ 2 T-Spn Killer Hogs AP Rub
- ✓ 2 T-Spn Mexican Style Seasoning
- ✓ **For the topping:**
- ✓ ¼ cup Mexican Blend Shredded Cheese
- ✓ sliced jalapeños

- ✓ Mexican Style Seasoning
- ✓ 3 Tbl-Spn Killer Hogs AP Rub
- ✓ 2 Tbl-Spn Chili Powder
- ✓ 2 Tbl-Spn Paprika
- ✓ 2 T-Spn Cumin
- ✓ ½ teaspoon Granulated Onion
- ✓ ¼ teaspoon Cayenne Pepper
- ✓ ¼ teaspoon Chipotle Chili Pepper ground
- ✓ ¼ teaspoon Oregano

INSTRUCTIONS

1. Preheat smoker or flame broil for roundabout cooking at 350^0
2. Join fixings in a big bowl and spot in a cast to press skillet
3. Top with Mexican Blend destroyed cheddar and cuts of jalapeno's
4. Spot iron skillet on flame broil mesh and cook until cheddar hot and bubbly and the top has seared
5. Marginally about 25mins.
6. Serve warm with enormous corn chips (scoops), tortilla chips, or your preferred vegetables for plunging.

CAJUN TURKEY CLUB

Prep Time: 5mins Cook Time: 10mins Total Times: 15mins   Serving: 3

INGREDIENTS

- ✓ 1 3lbs Turkey Breast
- ✓ 1 stick Butter (melted)
- ✓ 8oz Chicken Broth
- ✓ 1 Tbl-Spn Killer Hogs Hot Sauce
- ✓ 1/4 cup Malcolm's King Craw Seasoning
- ✓ 8 Pieces to Thick Sliced Bacon
- ✓ 1 cup Brown Sugar
- ✓ 1 head Green Leaf Lettuce
- ✓ 1 Tomato (sliced)
- ✓ 6 slices Toasted Bread

- ✓ 1/2 cup Cajun Mayo
- ✓ 1 cup Mayo
- ✓ 1 Tbl-Spn Dijon Mustard
- ✓ 1 Tbl-Spn Killer Hogs Sweet Fire Pickles (chopped)
- ✓ 1 Tbl-Spn Horseradish
- ✓ 1/2 tsp Malcolm's King Craw Seasoning
- ✓ 1 tsp Killer Hogs Hot Sauce
- ✓ Pinch of Salt & Black Pepper to taste

INSTRUCTIONS

1. Get ready pellet smoker for backhanded cooking at 325^0 utilizing your preferred wood pellets for enhancing.

2. Join dissolved margarine, chicken stock, hot sauce, and 1 Tbl-Spn of Cajun Seasoning in a blending bowl. Infuse the blend into the turkey bosom scattering the infusion destinations for even inclusion.

3. Shower the outside of the turkey bosom with a Vegetable cooking splash and season with Malcolm's King Craw Seasoning.

4. Spot the turkey bosom on the smoker and cook until the inside temperature arrives at 165^0. Utilize a moment read thermometer to screen temp during the cooking procedure.

5. Consolidate darker sugar and 1 teaspoon of King Craw in a little bowl. Spread the bacon with the sugar blend and spot on a cooling rack.

6. Cook the bacon for 12 to 15mins or until darker. Make certain to turn the bacon part of the way through for cooking.

7. Toast the bread, cut the tomatoes dainty, and wash/dry the lettuce leaves.

8. At the point when the turkey bosom arrives at 165 Take it from the flame broil and rest for 15mins. Take the netting out from around the bosom and cut into slender cuts.

9. To cause the sandwich: To slather Cajun Mayo* on the toast, stack on a few cuts of turkey bosom, lettuce, tomato, and bacon. Include another bit of toast and rehash a similar procedure. Include the top bit of toast slathered with more Cajun mayo, cut the sandwich into equal parts and appreciate.

GRILLED APPLE CRISP

Prep Time: 15mins Cook Time: 20mins Total Times:
35mins   Serving: 4

INGREDIENTS

- ✓ 3 Whole Apples
- ✓ Lemon Juice
- ✓ ½ C Granola Cereal
- ✓ 1 Tb Pumpkin Pie Spice
- ✓ 1 Tb. Maple Syrup
- ✓ 1 ½ Tb heaping Brown Sugar
- ✓ ½ Stick Butter
- ✓ 2 Tb Pecan Chips
- ✓ Handful of Craisins

INSTRUCTIONS

1. Preheat your Grilla or Silverbac to 400⁰. After washing
   apples, cut in half and trim a little off of the backside so

they sit flat. Core the middle of each half and set aside on a tray.

2. In a large bowl, combine the apple filling: granola, spice, syrup, and brown sugar. Add butter, pecans, and Craisins. Fill each apple with the mixture, piling on high. Put into the Grilla for 30mins until the apples are soft. Serve alone or paired with a scoop of ice cream.

QUICK N' EASY PEAR COBBLER

Prep Time: 15mins Cook Time: 60mins Total Times:

75mins   Serving: 8

INGREDIENTS

- ✓ 2 Large Cans Pear Halves in Syrup
- ✓ 1 C Flour
- ✓ 1 C Whole Milk
- ✓ 1 C Sugar
- ✓ ½ Tsp. vanilla extract
- ✓ Non to Stick Spray
- ✓ 1 Stick butter
- ✓ Cranberries
- ✓ Brown Sugar

INSTRUCTIONS

1. Preheat Grilla to 400⁰. While it's heating, whisk together flour, milk, sugar, and vanilla extract in a large bowl. Spray your baking dish with nonstick spray, or grease pan in

butter. Place one stick of butter in the bottom of greased pan, then put in the Grilla, Silverbac, or Kong.

2. After a few moments, the butter will melt. Remove pan and cover bottom of pan with the melted butter. Pour batter into pan. Place halved pears on top of the batter in an organized fashion, then top pears with a handful of cranberries. Sprinkle brown sugar over entire pan.

3. Put into the Grilla at 400⁰ for 40mins, or until top is golden brown. Let cool 15 to 20mins before serving.

JUICY LOOSEY CHEESEBURGER

Prep Time: 10mins Cook Time: 10mins Total Times: 20mins   Serving: 6

INGREDIENTS

- ✓ 2 lbs ground beef
- ✓ 1 egg beaten
- ✓ 1 C dry bread crumbs
- ✓ 3 TB evaporated milk
- ✓ 2 TB Worcestershire sauce
- ✓ 1 TB Grilla Grills All Purpose Rub
- ✓ 4 slices of cheddar cheese
- ✓ 4 buns

INSTRUCTIONS

1. Start by consolidating the hamburger, egg, dissipated milk, Worcestershire and focus on a bowl. Utilize your hands to blend well. Partition this blend into 4 equivalent parts. At that point take every one of the 4 sections and partition

them into equal parts. Take every one of these little parts and smooth them. The objective is to have 8 equivalent level patties that you will at that point join into 4 burgers.

2. When you have your patties smoothed, place your cheddar in the center and afterward place the other patty over this and firmly squeeze the sides to seal. You may even need to push the meat back towards the inside a piece to shape a marginally thicker patty. The patties ought to be marginally bigger than a standard burger bun as they will recoil a bit of during cooking.

3. Preheat your Kong to 300^0.

4. Keep in mind during flame broiling that you fundamentally have two meager patties, one on each side, so the cooking time ought not to have a place. You will cook these for 5 to 8mins per side—closer to 5mins on the off chance that you favor an uncommon burger or more towards 8mins in the event that you like a well to done burger.

5. At the point when you flip the burgers, take a toothpick and penetrate the focal point of the burger to permit steam to getaway. This will shield you from having a hit to out or having a visitor who gets a jaw consume from liquid cheddar as they take their first nibble.

6. Toss these on a pleasant roll and top with fixings that supplement whatever your burgers are loaded down with.

NO FLIP BURGERS

Prep Time: 30mins Cook Time: 30mins Total Times: 60mins   Serving: 2

INGREDIENTS

- ✓ Ground Beef Patties
- ✓ Grilla Grills Beef Rub
- ✓ Choice of Cheese
- ✓ Choice of Toppings
- ✓ Pretzel Buns

INSTRUCTIONS

1. To start, you'll need to begin with freezing yet not solidified meat patties. This will help guarantee that you don't overcook your burgers. Liberally sprinkle on our Beef Rub or All to Purpose Rub and delicately knead into the two sides of the patty. As another option, you can likewise season with salt and pepper and some garlic salt.

2. Preheat your Silverbac to 250° Fahrenheit and cook for about 45mins. Contingent upon the thickness of your burgers you will need to keep an eye on them after around 30 to 45mins, yet there's no compelling reason to flip. For a medium to uncommon burger, we recommend cooking to about 155°.

3. After the initial 30 to 40mins, in the event that you like liquefied cheddar on your burger feel free to mix it up. Close your barbecue back up and let them wrap up for another 10mins before evacuating. For an additional punch of flavor, finish your burger off with a sprinkle of Grilla Grill's Gold 'N Bold sauce. Appreciate!

JUICEY LOOSEY SMOKEY BURGER

Prep Time: 30mins Cook Time: 30mins Total Times: 60mins   Serving: 2

INGREDIENTS

- ✓ 80/20 beef
- ✓ 1/3 pound per burger
- ✓ Cheddar cheese
- ✓ Grilla AP Rub
- ✓ Salt
- ✓ Freshly Ground Black Pepper
- ✓ Hamburger Bun
- ✓ BBQ Sauce

INSTRUCTIONS

1. Split every 1/3 pound of meat, which is 2.66 ounces per half.

2. Level out one half to roughly six inches plate. Put wrecked of American cheddar, leaving 1/2 inch clear.
3. Put another portion of the meat on top, and seal edges. Rehash for all burgers.
4. Sprinkle with Grilla AP rub, salt, and pepper flame broil seasonings.
5. Smoke at 250 for 50mins. No compelling reason to turn.
6. Apply smokey Dokey BBQ sauce, ideally a mustard-based sauce like Grilla Gold and Bold, or Sticky Fingers Carolina Classic. Cook for an extra 10 mins, or to favored doneness.

CHIPOTLE TURKEY BURGERS

***Prep Time: 5mins Cook Time: 35mins Total Times:
40mins   Serving: 4***

INGREDIENTS

- ✓ 2 lb. Ground Turkey
- ✓ ½ C Onion Chopped and Sauteed
- ✓ 3 TBS Fresh Chopped Cilantro
- ✓ 2 chipotle chile in adobo sauce
- ✓ Finely chopped 2 tsp Garlic Powder
- ✓ 2 tsp onion powder
- ✓ 3 TBS Grilla Beef Rub
- ✓ 8 slices pepper jack cheese
- ✓ 8 hamburger buns

INSTRUCTIONS

1. Finely hack the onion. Spot turkey, onion, cilantro, chile pepper, garlic powder, onion powder, and Grilla Beef Rub in a massive bowl. Utilize your arms to combination nicely and structure into 8 patties.

161

2. Preheat either your Silverbac, Kong, or Grilla to 375^0. Cook the turkey burgers till they attain in any event 165^0. Cook time may be directed by using the thickness of burgers, but, keep in mind approximately 45min of prepare dinner time.

3. Utilize a little, profoundly precise thermometer, as an example, a Thermopop to test the inward temp. Try not to confide inside the vibe of the patties, you have to prepare dinner them till they arrive at one hundred sixty five to keep a strategic distance from any troubles. Just before the patties are Takeled from the flame broil, pinnacle with the cheddar and serve. On the off danger which you are hoping to keep all of the carbs out of the dish, avoid the bun and consume it like burger steak with sautéed onions and mushrooms.

4. In the occasion which you want fewer carbs but something nonetheless hand held, those are high-quality in a wrap with some farm dressing and tomato and lettuce. Our personal considered one of a kind Gold n Bold is an excellent mixing with these burgers too.

BREAD PUDDING

Prep Time: 15mins Cook Time: 45mins Total Times: 60mins   Serving: 4

INGREDIENTS

- ✓ 8 stale donuts
- ✓ 3 eggs
- ✓ 1 cup milk
- ✓ 1 cup heavy cream
- ✓ 1/2 cup brown sugar
- ✓ 1 tsp vanilla
- ✓ 1 pinch salt

BLUEBERRY
COMPOTE

- ✓ 1 pint blueberries

- ✓ 2/3 cup granulated sugar
- ✓ 1/4 cup water
- ✓ 1 lemon

OAT TOPPING

- ✓ 1 cup quick oats
- ✓ 1/2 cup brown sugar
- ✓ 1 tsp flour
- ✓ 2 to 3 tbsp room temperature butter

INSTRUCTIONS

1. Warmth your Grilla Grill to 350⁰.

2. Cut your doughnuts into 6 pieces for every doughnut and put it in a safe spot. Blend your eggs, milk, cream, darker sugar, vanilla, and salt in a bowl until it's everything fused. Spot your doughnuts in a lubed 9 by 13 container at that point pour your custard blend over the doughnuts. Press down on the doughnuts to guarantee they get covered well and absorb the juices.

3. In another bowl, consolidate your oats, dark colored sugar, flour and gradually join the spread with your hand until the blend begins to cluster up like sand. When that is prepared, sprinkle it over the highest point of the bread pudding and toss it on the barbecue around 40 to 45mins until it gets decent and brilliant dark-colored.

4. While the bread pudding is preparing, place your blueberries into a skillet over medium-high warmth and begin to cook them down so the juices begin to stream. When that occurs, include your sugar and water and blend well. Diminish the warmth to drug low and let it cook down until it begins to thicken up. Right when the blend begins to thicken, pizzazz your lemon and add the get-up-and-go to the blueberry compote and afterward cut your lemon down the middle and squeeze it into the blend. What you're left with is a tasty, splendid compote that is ideal for the sweetness of the bread pudding.

5. Watch out for your bread pudding around the 40 to 50mins mark. The blend will, in any case, shake a piece in

the middle however will solidify as it stands once you pull it off. You can pull it early on the off chance that you like your bread pudding more sodden however to me, the ideal bread pudding will be more dim with some caramelization yet will at present have dampness too!

6. Presently this is the point at which I'd snatch an attractive bowl, toss a pleasant aiding of bread pudding in there then top it off with the compote and a stacking scoop of vanilla bean frozen yogurt at that point watch faces light up. In addition to the fact that this is an amazingly beautiful dish, the flavor will take you out. Destined to be an enormous hit in your family unit. Give it a shot and express gratitude toward me later!

7. What's more, as usual, ensure you snap a photo of your manifestations and label us in your dishes! We'd love to include your work!

SMOKED CHOCOLATE BACON PECAN PIE

***Prep Time: 1hr 45mins Cook Time: 45mins Total
Times: 2hrs 30mins   Serving: 8***

INGREDIENTS

- ✓ 4 eggs
- ✓ 1 cup chopped pecans
- ✓ 1 Tbl-Spn of vanilla
- ✓ ½ cup semi to sweet chocolate chips
- ✓ ½ cup dark corn syrup
- ✓ ½ cup light corn syrup
- ✓ ¾ cup bacon (crumbled)
- ✓ ¼ cup bourbon

- ✓ 4 Tbl-Spn or ¼ cup of butter
- ✓ ½ cup brown sugar
- ✓ ½ cup white sugar
- ✓ 1 Tbl-Spn cornstarch
- ✓ 1 package refrigerated pie dough
- ✓ 16 oz heavy cream
- ✓ ¾ cup white sugar
- ✓ ¼ cup bacon
- ✓ 1 Tbl-Spn vanilla

INSTRUCTIONS

Pie:

1. Carry Smoker to 350⁰.

2. Blend 4 Tbl-Spn spread, ½ cup darker sugar, and ½ cup white sugar in blending bowl.

3. In a different bowl, blend 4 eggs and 1 Tbl-Spn cornstarch together and add to blender.

4. Include ½ cup dull corn syrup, ½ cup light corn syrup, ¼ cup whiskey, 1 cup slashed walnuts, 1 cup bacon, and 1 Tbl-Spn vanilla to blend.

5. Spot pie batter in 9-inch pie skillet.

6. Daintily flour mixture.

7. Uniformly place ½ cup chocolate contributes pie dish.

8. Take blend into the pie dish.

9. Smoke at 350⁰ for 40mins or until the focus is firm.

10. Cool and top with bacon whipped cream.

Bacon whipped Cream:

11. Consolidate fixings (16 oz substantial cream, ¾ cup white sugar, ¼ cup bacon tofinely cleaved, and 1 Tbl-Spn vanilla) and mix at rapid until blend thickens. This formula can be separated into 6mins pie container or custard dishes or filled in as one entire pie.

BACON SWEET POTATO PIE

Prep Time: 15mins Cook Time: 50mins Total Times: 65mins   Serving: 8

INGREDIENTS

- ✓ 1 pound 3 ounces sweet potatoes
- ✓ 1 1/4 cups plain yogurt
- ✓ ¾ cup packed, dark brown sugar
- ✓ ½ teaspoon of cinnamon
- ✓ ¼ teaspoon of nutmeg
- ✓ 5 egg yolks
- ✓ ¼ teaspoon of salt
- ✓ 1 (up to 9 inch) deep dish, frozen pie shell
- ✓ 1 cup chopped pecans, toasted
- ✓ 4 strips of bacon, cooked and diced
- ✓ 1 Tbl-Spn maple syrup
- ✓ Optional: Whipped topping

INSTRUCTIONS

1. In the first region, 3D shapes the potatoes right into a steamer crate and sees into a good-sized pot of stew water. Ensure the water is not any nearer than creeps from the base of the bushel. When steamed for 20mins, pound with a potato masher and installed a safe spot.

2. While your flame broil is preheating, location the sweet potatoes within the bowl of a stand blender and beat with the oar connection.

3. Include yogurt, dark colored sugar, cinnamon, nutmeg, yolks, and salt, to flavor, and beat until very a whole lot joined. Take this hitter into the pie shell and see onto a sheet dish. Sprinkle walnuts and bacon on pinnacle and bathe with maple syrup.

4. Heat for 45 to 60mins or until the custard arrives at 165 to 180^0. Take out from fish fry and funky. Keep refrigerated within the wake of cooling.

CHEESY CORN O'SHANE

Prep Time: 10mins Cook Time: 50mins Total Times: 60mins   Serving: 12

INGREDIENTS

- ✓ 52 oz. frozen corn
- ✓ 3 to 4 cup shredded cheese
- ✓ 1 brick cream cheese
- ✓ 6 strips of bacon
- ✓ ½ onion diced
- ✓ ½ red bell pepper
- ✓ ½ orange pepper diced
- ✓ Salt
- ✓ Pepper

INSTRUCTIONS

1. Cook bacon and chop. Use bacon grease to sauté the peppers and onion. Combine all ingredients in a pan including salt and pepper to taste. Smoke between 275 to

350 for 1hr to 2hrs or until cheese is melted. Stir every 30mins to ensure the cream cheese is combined.

BACON WRAPPED JALAPENO POPPERS

Prep Time: 25mins Cook Time: 25mins Total Times: 50mins   Serving: 12

INGREDIENTS

- ✓ Jalapeños
- ✓ Pimento Cheese
- ✓ Bacon
- ✓ Grilla Grills All Purpose Rub
- ✓ Gloves (optional)

INSTRUCTIONS

1. To begin with, take a gourmet expert's blade and slash off the highest point of the jalapeños. To abstain from getting the fiery oils on your fingers, we prescribe wearing a couple of elastic gloves. When the tops are hacked off, locate the most extensive part and make a cut longwise.

2. Next, take a paring blade to Take the seeds. You can desert a few seeds on the off chance that you need your poppers to have additional warmth. At that point, include your pimento cheddar spread into the emptied to out jalapeño. Finish this off with a sprinkle of the Grilla Grill's All to Purpose Rub.

3. Next, snatch a bit of bacon to fold over the jalapeño. Begin moving at the wide end and move until the bacon arrives at the base of the far edge. Utilize a toothpick to verify the bacon and afterward place the wrapped poppers onto a wire rack.

4. Preheat Silverbac to 275^0 Fahrenheit and cook for 45mins. Check part of the way through, yet there is no compelling reason to flip.

5. Evacuate your jalapeño poppers, let them cool for several mins and appreciate!

BACON SWEET POTATO PIE

Prep Time: 15mins Cook Time: 55mins Total Times:
70mins   Serving: 8

INGREDIENTS

- ✓ 1 pound 3 ounces sweet potatoes, peeled and cubed
- ✓ 1 1/4 cups plain yogurt
- ✓ ¾ cup packed, dark brown sugar
- ✓ ½ teaspoon of cinnamon
- ✓ ¼ teaspoon of nutmeg
- ✓ 5 egg yolks

- ✓ ¼ teaspoon of salt
- ✓ 1 (9 to inch) deep dish, frozen pie shell
- ✓ 1 cup chopped pecans, toasted
- ✓ 4 strips of bacon, cooked and diced
- ✓ 1 Tbl-Spn maple syrup
- ✓ Optional: Whipped topping

INSTRUCTIONS

1. First, cube the potatoes into a steamer basket and place into a large pot of simmer water. Make sure the water is no closer than two inches from the bottom of the basket. Once

steamed for 20mins, mash with a potato masher and set aside.

2. Now it's time to fire up your grill! Choose your Grilla Grill of choice.

3. While your grill is preheating, place the sweet potatoes in the bowl of a stand mixer and beat with the paddle attachment. Add yogurt, brown sugar, cinnamon, nutmeg, yolks, and salt, to taste, and beat until well combined. Pour this batter into the pie shell and place onto a sheet pan. Sprinkle pecans and bacon on top and drizzle with maple syrup.

4. Bake for 45 to 60mins or until the custard reaches 165 to 180^0. Remove from grill and cool. Keep refrigerated after cooling.

GRILLED PINEAPPLE WITH BROWN SUGAR GLAZE

Prep Time: 5mins Cook Time: 8mins Total Times: 13mins   Serving: 6

INGREDIENTS

- ✓ 1 fresh pineapple
- ✓ ¾ stick butter
- ✓ ¾ C brown sugar

INSTRUCTIONS

1. In a bowl, soften the butter slowly until melted. Add the brown sugar and stir quickly to combine. This will take aminsute or so for the sugar to absorb. Preheat your Kong to 350⁰.

2. Take a knife and peel your pineapple, slicing into ¾ to inch slices. Place the slices on your Kong and let cook about 5 to 7mins per side. You are looking just to get some good color

and grill marks on the first side before flipping and repeating.

3. Once done, remove pineapple slices and quickly brush the butter mixture on each side of the pineapple. Serve the brown sugar pineapple quickly.

GAME

CAJUN CRAB STUFFED SHRIMP AND JICAMA CORN SALAD

Prep Time: 20mins Cook Time: 0mins Total Times: 20mins   Serving: 4

INGREDIENTS

- ✓ Stuffed shrimp
- ✓ Lump crab meat
- ✓ Red onion
- ✓ Minced garlic Seasoning
- ✓ Lime juice
- ✓ Lime zest
- ✓ Jalapeno
- ✓ Ritz Crackers
- ✓ Bacon
- ✓ Grilled red onion and jalapeno

INSTRUCTIONS

1. Pick cartilage from the crab. Combine ingredients wrap with bacon. Grill till browned.

2. Remoulade Mayo, Chili sauce, Tiger sauce, Creole mustard, Lemon juice, Lemon zest, Scallions, Parsley,minsced celery,minsced garlic, Salt, Capers chopped, Salt, Black pepper. Combine all ingredients and chill Jicama corn salad.

3. Jicama, diced Corn on the cob, Black beans, Carrot, Scallions, Cilantro, Basil, Lime juice, Lime zest, Cumin Red bell pepper, Grill red pepper and corn on the cob.

4. Rinse black beans. Combine ingredients and chill.

CHAR SIU BABY BACK RIBS

Prep Time: 2hrs Cook Time: 1hr Total Times: 3hrs
Serving: 6

INGREDIENTS

MARINADE

- ✓ 1/3 c hoisin sauce
- ✓ 1/3 c soy sauce
- ✓ 2 Tbsp mirin
- ✓ 2 Tbsp honey
- ✓ 2 Tbsp light brown sugar
- ✓ 1 Tbsp Sambal Chili Paste
- ✓ 1/2 Tbsp Sesame Oil
- ✓ 1/2 Tbsp Chili Oil
- ✓ 1/2 tsp Chinese 5 spice seasoning
- ✓ 3/4 tsp red food coloring
- ✓ 3 cloves garlic, minsced fine

BASTING LIQUID

- ✓ 1/4 c hoisin
- ✓ 1/4 c soy sauce
- ✓ 3 Tbsp honey
- ✓ 1 Tbsp sesame oil
- ✓ 1 Tbsp mirin
- ✓ 1 tsp red miso paste
- ✓ 1 tsp sambal chili paste

GARNISH

- ✓ Toasted Sesame Seeds
- ✓ Scallions

INSTRUCTIONS

1. Directions: Combine all marinade fixings, and race to join.

2. Slice child back ribs into 2 bone areas. This builds the surface territory for the marinade to give more flavor

3. Spot ribs and marinade in a hurdle to top back, evacuating however much air as could be expected, and marinate for in any event 4Hrs. Marinate medium-term if conceivable.

4. Evacuate ribs and hold marinade.

5. Spot ribs on smoker at 250F. Try not to contact the principal 2Hrs.

6. Join saved marinade and extra treating fluid fixings into a sauce skillet. Bring to a stew, mixing once in a while, for 10mins. Take out from the heat.

7. At the 2hrs mark, treat ribs with seasoning fluid, and rehash each 30mins, until ribs are delicate roughly 4Hrs.

8. Cut ribs segments into singular ribs, embellish with sesame seeds and scallions.

CITRUS HERB SALT

Prep Time: 15mins Cook Time: 3hrs Total Times: 3hrs 15mins   Serving: 4

INGREDIENTS

- ✓ 1 C high to quality, coarse kosher salt
- ✓ 2 tsp rosemary
- ✓ 2 tsp thyme
- ✓ 2 tsp granulated garlic
- ✓ 2 Limes tozested
- ✓ 1 Lemon tozested

INSTRUCTIONS

1. Start with a high to quality salt. Don't modest out and get the iodized salt—you truly need a decent, coarse salt for this.

2. Include all herbs. Over a different bowl, pizzazz the lemon and two limes (zesting the citrus over the salt blend could add an excessive amount of fluid to the condition).

3. Add the pizzazz to the salt and herb blend, blend well and store in dashing to top pack.

4. For a principal couple of days, shake up the pack once every day to guarantee every one of the fixings persuades an opportunity to be dried out by the salt.

5. This will permit the salt to ingest every one of the kinds of herbs and pizzazz. Use varying.

CORNED BEEF PASTRAMI

Prep Time: 5days Cook Time: 3hrs Total Times: 0mins Serving: 16

INGREDIENTS

- ✓ 3 tbsp. coarse ground pepper
- ✓ 2 tbsp. granulated garlic
- ✓ 2 tbsp. onion flakes
- ✓ 2 tbsp. ancho chili powder
- ✓ Ancho expresso rub

INSTRUCTIONS

1. Rinse the meat in chilly water and afterward absorb cold water for 24hrs, changing the water each 6hrs to pull a greater amount of the salt and fix from the meat.

2. Remove from the water and pat dry with a towel. Apply the rub fixings and put in a safe spot while the smoker heats up. Cook at 250^0 until the inward temperature hits 150^0. This should take 3 to 4hrs.

3. Wrap in either foil or butcher paper and keep cooking until the inner temp arrives at 185 to 195^0. This should take another 2Hrs around.

DINO BONES BEEF SHORT RIBS

***Prep Time: 10mins Cook Time: 8hrs Total Times:
8hrs 10mins   Serving: 4***

INGREDIENTS

BRAISE

- ✓ 1 Cup Beef Broth or Stock
- ✓ 1 Cup Red Wine
- ✓ ¼ Cup Worcestershire Sauce
- ✓ 2 Tbsp. Butter

SPRITZ

- ✓ 1 Cup Apple Cider Vinegar
- ✓ 1 Cup Apple Juice

INSTRUCTIONS

1. To start with, score the uncooked ribs and cut back off any
   excess or not to uniform meat. When cut, pour olive oil
   over the film side of the meat. Next, coat ribs in our Grilla
   Grills Beef Rub and spread equally.

2. In a profound to dish heating skillet, consolidate meat stock, red wine, Worcestershire sauce, and margarine to make the braise. In a little bowl or splash bottle, join apple juice vinegar and squeezed apple to make cooking spritz.

3. Preheat Grilla or Silverbac to 250⁰ Fahrenheit and spot hamburger ribs legitimately on the rack. Consistently splash ribs with the spritz blend. Leave on the flame broil for generally threeHrs.

4. When cooked, Take the ribs and spot them meat side down in the braising blend. Seal dish firmly with tin foil and spot back on the flame broil for an extra 2 to 2 ½Hrs or until the interior temperature arrives at 200⁰.

5. Pull from the flame broil and flip ribs so the meat is looking up. Sprinkle with meat rub and let sit until cool.

6. Cut, serve, and appreciate!

RATATOUILLE ORIGINAL RECIPE WITH HALLOUMI CHEESE

Prep Time: 20mins Cook Time: 2hrs Total Times: 2hrs 20mins   Serving: 8

INGREDIENTS

- ✓ 2 Tbsp Olive Oil
- ✓ 1 Tbsp Dried Roasted Garlic
- ✓ 1 Tbsp Herbs de Province
- ✓ 1 Jar Marinara
- ✓ Salt & Pepper to taste
- ✓ 2 Green Zucchini's
- ✓ 2 Yellow Zucchini's
- ✓ 2 Red Onions
- ✓ 2 Sweet Potatoes
- ✓ 4 Roma Tomatoes
- ✓ 6 Large Cap (stuffing) Mushrooms
- ✓ 2 Packages Halloumi Cheese

INSTRUCTIONS

1. Slice all vegetables and cheese 1/4 inch thick.
2. Add a jar of marinara to a 10" round (or square) baking dish, spreading evenly.

3. Place one of each vegetable including cheese together until the pan is full.

4. Drizzle with olive oil.

5. Season with salt and pepper, crushed roasted garlic and herbs de province.

6. Set Grill to 225^0 and bake uncovered for 2Hrs.

7. Increase temp to 375^0 for another 30 to 45mins until lightly browned.

8. Remove and serve hot or cold as a fantastic fall harvest side dish.

9. Enjoy!

GOLD 'N' BOLD TAILGATE CHICKEN SKEWERS

Prep Time: 5mins Cook Time: 70mins Total Times: 75mins   Serving: 8

INGREDIENTS

- ✓ 2 lbs Cubed Chicken
- ✓ 1/3 Cup Grilla Grills Gold 'N' Bold Sauce
- ✓ 1 1/2 Teaspoon of Curry Powder (Optional)
- ✓ Skewer Sticks
- ✓ 3 T-Spn of Grilla Grills All Purpose Rub

INSTRUCTIONS

1. After your chicken has been cubed add your dry ingredients. If you want a spicier end product, use more curry powder. If spice is not your thing, feel free to omit it entirely. Toss until thoroughly coated.

2. Next, add the Gold 'N' Bold Sauce, and mix until chicken is coated.

3. Set this aside in the refrigerator. The colder the chicken is, the easier it is to slide on the skewers.

4. Once your chicken is skewered, preheat your Grilla Grill to 350^0. Make sure to take your time when threading the chicken and space the pieces evenly.

5. Cook at 350 for roughly 12 to 15mins or until chicken reaches personal preference of doneness. Must reach an internal temperature of at least 160^0 Fahrenheit.

6. Once the chicken is almost to your target temp, feel free to brush on an additional layer of Gold 'N' Bold sauce if you'd like an extra kick of flavor.

GRILLA SAVORY BBQ RANCH DIP

Prep Time: 20mins Cook Time: 30mins Total Times: 50mins   Serving: 6

INGREDIENTS

- ✓ 2 C sour cream
- ✓ 3 TB Grilla BBQ sauce
- ✓ 1 TB Grilla AP Rub
- ✓ 1 packet Hidden Valley Ranch dressing mix

INSTRUCTIONS

1. Combine all ingredients in a large bowl and watch it disappear.

GRILLA GRILLED BOLOGNA

Prep Time: 10mins Cook Time: 4hrs Total Times: 4hrs 10mins   Serving: 20

INGREDIENTS

- ✓ 10 to lb stick of bologna
- ✓ 1 C Grilla AP Rub
- ✓ 1 bottle Grilla BBQ Sauce

INSTRUCTIONS

1. Preheat pellet flame broil to 225⁰. Take the wrapper from the bologna and cut it into equal parts length to savvy. Liberally cover the bologna on all sides with rub. Toss on the Grilla Grill and cook for 3Hrs.

2. At 3Hrs, raise your pit temperature to about 375⁰ and begin covering the outside with your sauce. Two coats ought to do it with 15mins of pit time between each coat. Let the sauce caramelize a piece on the last cover and afterward Take from the barbecue.

GRILLED LONDON BROIL FLANK STEAK

Prep Time: 5mins Cook Time: 15mins Total Times: 20mins   Serving: 6

INGREDIENTS

- ✓ 3 TB crumbled blue cheese
- ✓ 2 TB butter
- ✓ 1 tsp chives
- ✓ ¼ C Grilla AP Rub
- ✓ 1 2 to lb beef flank steak
- ✓ 2 TB olive oil

INSTRUCTIONS

1. Preheat Silverbac to 225⁰. In a bowl mix the blue cheese, butter, and chives and set aside. Rub the steak with olive oil, coating both sides and then dust with the rub. Place meat on a pellet grill, cooking 10 to 15mins per side or to desired doneness. We recommend not going past medium

and even prefer cooking to just medium to rare (an internal temp of 130^0).

2. Remove from the Silverbac, slice across the grain into thin strips, and top with a dollop of the blue cheese butter mixture.

GRILLED MAHI MAHI FISH TACOS WITH CREAMY CHIPOTLE SAUCE

Prep Time: 15mins Cook Time: 5mins Total Times: 20mins   Serving: 6

INGREDIENTS

- ✓ 2 to 3 lb. Mahi Mahi
- ✓ 3 TB Grilla AP Rub
- ✓ 8 flour or corn tortillas
- ✓ ¼ head small green, shredded
- ✓ 1 medium tomato, chopped
- ✓ 2 limes cut into wedges

CHIPOTLE SAUCE

- ✓ ½ C mayonnaise
- ✓ 1/3 C plain Greek yogurt
- ✓ ½ tsp dried oregano
- ✓ ¼ tsp ground cumin
- ✓ ¼ tsp dried dill
- ✓ 1 canned chipotle chile in adobo sauce + 1 tsp of the sauce
- ✓ salt and pepper to taste

INSTRUCTIONS

1. Start by making the chipotle sauce (can be made a day ahead, if you wish). Place all the ingredients in a blender and puree until smooth. Refrigerate until ready to use. Preheat your Grilla, Kong, or Silverbac to 300^0. Pat your fish dry with a paper towel, dust with the rub. Place the fish on the Grilla Grill and cook for 5 to 7mins per side. You may need more time if your fish is thick.

2. Serve fish on warm tortillas with the cabbage, onion, tomato and a generous dab of the chipotle sauce with a squeeze of lime.

GRILLED SALMON W/ HONEY SRIRACHA LIME GLAZE

Prep Time: 10mins Cook Time: 20mins Total Times: 30mins   Serving: 4

INGREDIENTS

- ✓ 4 - 6pieces of skinless salmon fillet.
- ✓ 1/3 C olive oil
- ✓ ¼ C Grilla AP Rub
- ✓ ¼ C honey
- ✓ 2 TB lime juice
- ✓ 2 TB Sriracha

INSTRUCTIONS

1. Utilize a paper towel to pat salmon dry. Brush fish with olive oil and residue with the rub. Preheat Grilla Grill to 300⁰. Spot fish on barbecue level to side up. When you have flame broil marks, flip the fish over.

2. It should just take around 5 to 8mins per side. You can check for barbecue stamps by lifting one corner of the fish with a spatula. Be delicate as the fish will turn out to be increasingly fragile as it cooks.

3. When you flip the fish, begin brushing the coating on. When the fish begins to feel firm and has flame broil blemishes on the two sides, it is finished. In the event that you like your salmon rarer, don't hesitate to pull it off the flame broil prior. You would prefer not to overcook it, however, the coating will help rescue any drier parts.

4. Serve the fish with the additional nectar sriracha salmon coating.

GRILLED THAI PEANUT STEAK

Prep Time: 30mins Cook Time: 10mins Total Times: 40mins   Serving: 8

INGREDIENTS

- ✓ Ribeye steak
- ✓ Salt
- ✓ Pepper
- ✓ Cavenders Greek seasoning
- ✓ Milk
- ✓ Peanut butter
- ✓ Rice wine vinegar
- ✓ Soy sauce
- ✓ Ginger
- ✓ Cilantro
- ✓ Scallions
- ✓ Peanuts

INSTRUCTIONS

1. Season your steak generously with genuine salt, dark pepper and schedules and flame broil to a medium to uncommon. While steak is cooking heat 1/4 cup milk, 1 tbsp nutty spread, 1 tsp soy, 1/2 tsp few mins ginger in a container. If necessary add more milk to thin sauce or progressively nutty spread to thicken.

2. When it's fused, include a scramble of rice wine vinegar. After your steak is cooked and permitted to sit 5mins, cut your steak, spoon on your sauce and top with hacked cilantro, scallion, and peanuts.

GUINNESS GRAVY GLAZE

***Prep Time: 15mins Cook Time: 45mins Total Times:
60mins   Serving: 4***

INGREDIENTS

- ✓ 2 bottles Guinness stout
- ✓ 1 can french onion soup
- ✓ ½ cup balsamic vinegar
- ✓ ¼ cup Worcestershire sauce
- ✓ ¼ cup beef broth concentrate
- ✓ 1 tbsp.minsced garlic
- ✓ 1 tbsp. tomato paste
- ✓ 1 tbsp. black peppercorns
- ✓ 1/3 cup brown sugar
- ✓ ½ tbsp. xanthan gum powder
- ✓ ½ stick salted Kerrygold butter

INSTRUCTIONS

1. Consolidate all fixings and warmth until stewing somewhat. Utilize a submersion blender or standard blender to mix all fixings until smooth. Set back in the container and keep on warming until the sauce begins to thicken.

2. When the sauce begins to cover a spoon well include the margarine and dissolve and keep mixing. Put aside to sprinkle over meat or to utilize it as a plunge once the meat is finished.

HERB CRUSTED PRIME RIB

Prep Time: 10mins Cook Time: 2hrs 30mins Total Times: 2hrs 40mins   Serving: 4

INGREDIENTS

- ✓ Whole Boneless Ribeye
- ✓ Butchers Twine
- ✓ Olive Oil
- ✓ 3/4 cup Tones Rosemary Garlic Seasoning
- ✓ 4 tbsp. Black Pepper
- ✓ 2 tbsp. Hazelnut Coffee
- ✓ 1 tbsp. Onion Powder
- ✓ 2 tbsp. Kosher Salt
- ✓ 1 tbsp. Cumin
- ✓ 2 tbsp. Brown Sugar

INSTRUCTIONS

1. Get ready prime rib flavoring one day ahead of time. Consolidate flavoring, pepper, espresso, powder, salt,

cumin, and sugar and spot clinched. Take silver skin from ribeye. Use butchers twine to envelop the prime rib by a roundabout shape. Coat with olive oil and apply it to season intensely.

2. Preheat Silverbac or Grilla to 225°F. Put your prime rib on the barbecue and smoke for 3 to 4Hrs until the inside is approx. 115°F to 120°F. Take prime rib and re to season as wanted. Warmth Silverbac to 500°F. Singe prime rib, moving edge each 3mins. Serve once the inside temperature at the middle arrives at 135°F.

3. Coating your prime rib with Grilla Horseradish sauce

HORSERADISH SAUCE

Prep Time: 2mins Cook Time: 2mins Total Times: 4mins   Serving: 12

INGREDIENTS

- ✓ 4 Tbl-Spn prepared horseradish in vinegar or 4oz jar
- ✓ 1 cup sour cream
- ✓ ½ cup milk
- ✓ ¼ cup mayonnaise
- ✓ 1 teaspoon kosher salt
- ✓ Zest of 1 lemon

INSTRUCTIONS

1. Mix horseradish, sour cream, milk, mayo, salt, and lemon in a bowl. Refrigerate at least 24Hrs before serving.

HOT BACON EXPLOSION

Prep Time: 15mins Cook Time: 3hrs Total Times: 3hrs 15mins   Serving: 8

INGREDIENTS

- ✓ 2 packages thick to cut bacon
- ✓ 1 package of Italian sausage
- ✓ ¼ C Formaggio blend cheese
- ✓ 3 - 6 jalapeños
- ✓ 1 package cream cheese
- ✓ ½ bottle BBQ Sauce
- ✓ 1 C Grilla AP Rub

INSTRUCTIONS

1. Wash, top and center your jalapenos. Utilizing an apparatus, for example, the "Pepper Whipper" truly accelerates this procedure. On the off chance that you've never observed a Pepper Whipper, it is the reasonable plastic instrument on the cutting board. They are cheap,

basic and simple to utilize and in the event that you do a lot of A.B.T.s, at that point you need one.

2. Spot cream cheddar in a bowl, either put in the microwave for several seconds to mollify or permit to sit out for 20 to 30mins on the counter to help in simpler blending. Include ¼ cup of the blended cheddar, 1.5 TBS of AP Rub and 3 TBS of Smokin Sauce to cream cheddar and blend well in a stand blender on the low setting.

3. Spot cheddar blends into a plastic zoom to top sack. Take one corner of the pack and funnel cheddar blend into jalapenos. Ensure you get the cheddar right to the base of each jalapeño.

4. Spread bacon out on cutting board, making a bacon weave. Coat finished weave with AP Rub.

5. Take housings out from whelps, combine the meat and afterward spread into one even layer on the bacon weave. Residue wiener with AP Rub and afterward sprinkle with Smokin' Sauce.

6. Slice the tip to off of one jalapeno. Spot it in weave/hotdog canvas and afterward place a jalapeno on either side of it. This will make one long jalapeño.

7. Move weave and frankfurter around the jalapenos framing a roll. Residue with more AP Rub.

8. Smoke on a 250 to degree Silverbac until inside temp comes to in any event 145⁰ or until you accomplish the immovability and shading you are searching for. Focus on

more straightforward warmth or cooking on the pit with the most warmth to guarantee the bacon gets completely cooked. Brush with Smokin' Sauce the last 15mins of cook time and include a second coat similarly as you are Takeling from the pit.

9. Let cool for in any event 25mins before cutting to permit the cream cheddar to cement once more. At that point appreciate.

HOT WINGS

Prep Time: 15mins Cook Time: 45mins Total Times: 1hr   Serving: 8

INGREDIENTS

- ✓ 10 lbs. chicken wings
- ✓ 1 bottle franks hot sauce
- ✓ 1 bottle zesty Italian dressing
- ✓ 1 cup Worcestershire sauce
- ✓ 1 cup Kikkoman teriyaki marinade
- ✓ 1/2 cup soy sauce.all to purpose seasoning (salt, pepper, garlic powder)
- ✓ Killer hogs dry rub

INSTRUCTIONS

1. Mix together hot sauce, Italian dressing, Worcestershire sauce, soy sauce in 2 1/2 gal ziplock bag, add wings, marinate overnight.
2. Heat grill to 250.

3. Put wings on sprayed Bradley racks, sprinkle both sides of wings with AP rub, repeat process with killer hogs rub, smoke for 60Secs, turn wings over and smoke for another 30 to 45mins.

4. Make sure internal temp is 165^0 or more.

5. Enjoy!

HOW TO TRIM A BRISKET

Prep Time: 20mins Cook Time: 8hrs 45mins Total Times: 1hr Serving: 8

INGREDIENTS

- ✓ Brisket
- ✓ Boning Knife/Chef's Knife
- ✓ Cutting Board
- ✓ Trash Bowl
- ✓ Patience

INSTRUCTIONS

1. Pick your Brisket
2. Give it a Rinse & Choose Your Knife
3. Plan Your Cuts
4. Start Trimming
5. Remove All of the Surface Fat
6. Cut Out the Point End Fat
7. Pause to Admire Your Work
8. Turn & Repeat

9. Get Ready to Season Your Brisket

10. Discard Excess Fat.

KICKIN' KY BOURBON JERKY

Prep Time: 15mins Cook Time: 4hrs Total Times: 4hrs 15mins   Serving: 6

INGREDIENTS

- ✓ 1/4 cup Bourbon
- ✓ 1 TBS Molasses
- ✓ 2 TBS Brown Sugar
- ✓ 1 TSP Black Pepper
- ✓ 1/4 cup Soy Sauce, Tamari
- ✓ 2 TBS Kongo Kick Sauce
- ✓ 1 TBS Grilla Beef Rub
- ✓ 2 TSP Red Pepper Flakes

INSTRUCTIONS

1. Makes enough for around 2lbs of cut meat. Meat can be presliced by your butcher. On the off chance that not utilizing presliced meat, at that point cut contrary to what would be expected and attempt to cut into 1/8 to 1/4 inch

cuts. Cooling your meat in the cooler for 15 to 20min preceding cutting will make cutting simpler.

2. Include all fixings with the exception of Grilla Beef into a bowl and blend. Add the blend to flash to top pack and include hamburger cuts.

3. Marinade 6hrs or medium-term. Take the meat out from marinade and channel well. Residue with Grilla Beef and Red Pepper Flakes (discretionary) as you put the cuts on the flame broil.

4. Set flame broil to 200^0 and smoke utilizing a solid pellet, for example, hickory until the cuts split however not break when bowed. Doneness involves individual inclination, however. To what extent this procedure takes will be dictated by mugginess noticeable all around and thickness of hamburger cuts.

5. Begin checking and pivoting the jerky at about the 2hr imprint to guarantee even drying out of the meat. When done permit jerky to cool and store in a water/air proof compartment. On the off chance that you live in a muggy situation consider putting away your jerky in the cooler.

LEMON GINGER GRILLED SHRIMP

Prep Time: 15mins Cook Time: 2hrs 15mins Total Times: 2hrs 30mins   Serving: 9

INGREDIENTS

- ✓ 3 lbs jumbo shrimp, peeled and deveined
- ✓ ½ C olive oil
- ✓ 2 tsp sesame oil
- ✓ ¼ C lemon juice
- ✓ 1 onion chopped
- ✓ 2 cloves garlic peeled
- ✓ 2 TB grated ginger root
- ✓ 2 TB cilantro
- ✓ 3 TB Grilla AP Rub
- ✓ 12 to 15 skewers

INSTRUCTIONS

1. To spare some time and exertion, utilize a blender or nourishment processor and include the olive oil, lemon juice, garlic, ginger, cilantro and rub and mix until smooth. Save a modest quantity of this blend for conclusive brushing.

2. Take the rest and fill a dish and include the shrimp, toss to cover and afterward cover and refrigerate for 1 to 2Hrs. Preheat Grilla to about 250⁰. String the shrimp on the sticks. Try to string through the tail and head region to keep them secure. Keep them all spread out a similar way to take into account flipping off the sticks. Discard remaining marinade.

3. Barbecue shrimp 3 to 4mins per side or until murky. Treat with staying held sauce. In the event that you need more shading on your shrimp, you can include 1 Tbl-Spn of BBQ sauce to your blend.

LOBSTER TAILS & HERB BUTTER

Prep Time: 10mins Cook Time: 10mins Total Times: 20mins   Serving: 2

INGREDIENTS

- ✓ Lobster Tails
- ✓ 1 lb. Butter
- ✓ ½ Cup Fresh Basil
- ✓ Olive Oil
- ✓ 1 tbspof Grilla Grills All Purpose Rub

INSTRUCTIONS

1. You'll begin by parting the lobster tails down the middle. Spot the lobster topsy turvy on your cutting board and utilizing a sharp culinary specialist's blade, slice through the center of the lobster. When you are through the primary layer, delicately air out it the remainder of the way.

2. Next, an emergency one pound of spread and empty it into a blending bowl. Join ½ cup new cleaved basil and include 1 Tbl-Spn of Grilla Grill's All to Purpose Rub in the event that you might want an additional punch to add more to taste. Combine and put in a safe spot.

3. Set the Kong to 275^0. Since the lobster will cook rapidly, think about utilizing a diffuser to cook over backhanded warmth. Utilize a brush to apply a layer of olive oil to every lobster tail directly before putting it on the flame broil. Likewise, brush on a layer of oil to your meshes where each tail will land.

4. Spot the lobster tail substance to side down and leave for an aggregate of about 5mins. You'll need to adhere close by to keep an eye on them about once consistently. The tails are done when you see a decent ruddy to orange shell shading and the meat turns smooth white.

5. Wrap up by garnish with the herb margarine and appreciate it!

O.G. YARD BIRD

Prep Time: 30mins Cook Time: 30mins Total Times: 60mins   Serving: 4

INGREDIENTS

- ✓ Tyson Whole Chicken
- ✓ Heath Riles Everyday Rub
- ✓ Heath Riles Honey Chipotle Rub
- ✓ Daigels Applewood Jalapeno Sauce
- ✓ Daigels Apple Heat Glaze

INSTRUCTIONS

1. Preheat O.G. to 350*.
2. Spatchcock chicken pulling back the skin from the breast to season.
3. Spray olive oil and apply Heath Riles everyday rub first coat, the apply Heath Riles Chipotle rub on top of that.
4. Place the bird in pit and mist with apple juice when needed.

5. When a bird hits 160 apply Daigels Jalapeno sauce and let sit for 10 to 15 in the pit.

6. After 10 to 15 apply glaze and let sit for 10mins in the pit.

7. Let the bird rest for 20mins.

8. Enjoy your O.G. yard bird.

NO WRAP RIBS

Prep Time: 20mins Cook Time: 3hrs Total Times: 3hrs 20mins   Serving: 4

INGREDIENTS

- ✓ 3 racks of St. Louis
- ✓ 1 Bottle Grilla Grills All Purpose Rub
- ✓ 1 Bottle Grills Beef Rub
- ✓ 1 Cup Apple Cider Vinegar or Apple Juice

INSTRUCTIONS

1. Take silver skin out from the ribs. Softly dust the front and posteriors of the ribs with AP Rub.

2. Spot ribs on a 250 to 265-degree flame broil. When an hour you will spritz the ribs and coat with a layer of rub. Toward the finish of hour 1 spritz and residue with Beef.

3. Hour 2 spritz and residue with AP.

4. Hour 3 spritz and residue with Beef.

5. As you are arriving at the finish of hour 4 the ribs ought to be near done. You can decide now on the off chance that you need to decrease or add sauce to the ribs as they are completing the cooking procedure.

6. Your ribs might be done when 3.5hrs relying upon thickness yet may take as long as 5hrs on the off chance that they are exceptionally thick. Simply utilize the twist test to decide delicacy. On the off chance that the rib twists and begins to split on the off chance that you get the full rack they are unquestionably done.

ORANGE VANILLA GRILLED FRENCH TOAST

Prep Time: 30mins Cook Time: 20mins Total Times: 50mins   Serving: 6

INGREDIENTS

- ✓ 8 slices day to old sourdough bread
- ✓ 4 eggs
- ✓ ¼ C milk
- ✓ ½ tsp vanilla extract
- ✓ 1 tsp ground cinnamon
- ✓ ¼ tsp ground nutmeg
- ✓ 2 TB sugar
- ✓ ¼ tsp orange zest

INSTRUCTIONS

1. In a huge bowl, whisk together the entirety of the fixings (other than bread) until it's all-around mixed. Spot the egg blend in a shallow bowl. Preheat the Grilla to 350⁰. Take

the bowl to your Grilla with you. Drench the primary bit of bread for around 5 seconds on each side, at that point place the doused bread on the pellet barbecue.

2. Continue including cuts of bread until they are all on. Flip the main piece after 3mins. As you flip the done side up, you can tidy with all the more crisp cinnamon and orange get-up-and-go. After another 2 to 3mins, the cut ought to be brilliant darker.

3. Take the flame-broiled toast out from Grilla and present with dissolved spread and warm maple syrup.

PINEAPPLE BOURBON GLAZED HAM

Prep Time: 10mins Cook Time: 2hrs 30mins Total Times: 2hrs 40mins   Serving: 16

INGREDIENTS

- ✓ Spiral Cut Ham or any pre to cooked ham
- ✓ 18 oz. Pineapple Preserves
- ✓ 1/3 cup Dark Molasses
- ✓ 1 cup Honey
- ✓ 1 cup Bourbon
- ✓ 1/2 cup Brown Sugar
- ✓ 1 tbsp. Ground Mustard
- ✓ 1/3c to 1/2c Grilla AP Rub

INSTRUCTIONS

1. Glaze: Combine over low heat and continue to stir for about 20min or until the glaze thickens. Remove from heat and let cool to continue thickening.

2. Ham: Smoke at 225° for 4 to 6hrs or until happy with color. Glaze every 10 to 15min during the final hour of smoking.

SALMON LOAF WITH DILL SAUCE

Prep Time: 20mins Cook Time: 50mins Total Times: 70mins   Serving: 4

INGREDIENTS

SALMON LOAF

- ✓ 1 lb. cooked salmon
- ✓ 1/2 c.minsced celery
- ✓ 1/ c.minsced onion
- ✓ 2 T. butter
- ✓ 1 tsp. kosher salt or 1/2 tsp table salt
- ✓ 2 eggs lightly beaten
- ✓ 1 rounded cup panko
- ✓ 2 T. lemon juice
- ✓ 2 T. chopped fresh dill

- ✓ 5 to 6 shakes Tabasco or Frank's hot sauce

DILL SAUCE

- ✓ 1/2 c. mayonnaise
- ✓ 1/2 c. yogurt tonot Greek
- ✓ 1 T. lemon juice
- ✓ 1 T. chopped capers
- ✓ 1 T. chopped fresh dill
- ✓ Hot sauce such as Tabasco to taste

INSTRUCTIONS

1. Sweat onion and celery in 2 T. margarine until delicate and cool marginally.

2. Then, piece your salmon into a bowl. (It's pleasant to have preplanned this from a past cook.) Added vegetables and every single residual fixing to bowl and blend in with a fork or hands.

3. Shower a bit of foil with oil and structure salmon blend into a portion for a move to the Grilla or oil a 9″x5″ container and press salmon blend into the skillet.

4. Warmth barbecue to 375⁰ while salmon portion comes back to the cooler to chill. Heat portion for an hour or until your ideal level of doneness.

5. Take a portion out from the Grilla and permit to rest 15 or 20mins. Cut and present with the Dill Caper sauce.

6. Sauce: Mix every one of the fixings in a little bowl. Alter flavoring to taste and chill while the salmon portion heats.

9 781914 025501